meditations

By the Author

Books
Creative Visualization
Creative Visualization Workbook
Living in the Light (with Laurel King)
Living in the Light Workbook
Reflections in the Light
Awakening
The Path of Transformation
The Four Levels of Healing
Creating True Prosperity
Developing Intuition

Audios
Creative Visualization
Creative Visualization Meditations
Living in the Light
Meditations
Relationships As Mirrors
The Path of Transformation
The Four Levels of Healing
Creating True Prosperity
Meditations for Creating True Prosperity
Developing Intuition

Videos
Creative Visualization Workshop
Living in the Light
The Path of Transformation

meditations

revised and expanded

Creative Visualization and Meditation Exercises to Enrich Your Life

⤜ SHAKTI GAWAIN ⤛

NATARAJ PUBLISHING
a division of

NEW WORLD LIBRARY
NOVATO, CALIFORNIA

Nataraj Publishing

a division of

New World Library
14 Pamaron Way
Novato, California 94949

Copyright © 1991, 2002 by Shakti Gawain

Cover design by Alexandra Graham
Text design and typography by Katie Blount
Author photograph by Susan Schelling

Library of Congress Cataloging-in-Publication Data
Gawain, Shakti
  Meditations : creative visualization and meditation exercises to enrich your life / By Shakti Gawain.— 1st rev. ed.
      p.   cm.
  ISBN 978-1-57731-235-2 (pbk. : alk. paper)
    1.   Meditation.   2.   Visualization.   3.   Self-actualization (Psychology)
I. Title.
  BF637.M4 G39 2002
    158.1'28—dc21   2002007501

Revised edition printed in September 2002
ISBN 978-1-57731-235-2
Printed in Canada on 100% postconsumer waster, recycled paper

10   9   8   7   6   5   4

Contents

Introduction to the Revised Edition

This book came about in a special way. Over the years, I recorded a series of guided meditations on audio cassette. Several people contacted my publisher and asked if there were transcriptions of the tapes — for various reasons, they preferred the written to the spoken word.

One of the first requests came from a group of older people who met regularly. Each time, a different person would lead the group, reading a meditation from one of my books to the others. They had gone through every meditation in my books, and now wanted transcriptions of the tapes so they could continue reading the meditations to each other.

These stories and requests were touching, and they prompted me to make transcriptions of the tapes.

Then several people at New World Library told me the transcriptions would make a beautiful book. All I needed to do was go through the text carefully and add or change as I saw fit. It was certainly one of my more effortless projects!

When it came time to do a new edition, we all felt that adding some more meditations would make the book even more complete, touching on so many different areas of our lives — from intuition, creativity, and spirituality to prosperity, relationships, and global healing.

There are several different ways this book can be used:

1. Sit down with a friend, or several friends, and appoint one person as a reader who guides the others through the meditations, like our friends the elders did.

2. Read through one of the meditations, alone, and then put your book down, close your eyes, and do your own version of the meditation.

3. Read through a bit of the meditation, relax and do it, and then read a bit more, relax and do it, and so on.

4. Record the meditations on cassette and lead yourself through them.

There is no right or wrong way to work with any of this. Any time you spend relaxing and doing these meditations is time well-spent.

I hope that these meditations will inspire and support you on your path of self-discovery.

Shakti Gawain
Summer 2002

Note to readers:
The ellipses (three or four dots ...) indicate
places to pause a bit.

meditations

Relaxation

This exercise is designed for very deep relaxation. Just as with learning any kind of new activity, such as riding a bicycle or running, it takes a while to train your body and mind to respond in a new way. The instructions given here will help you achieve a balanced and effective relaxation response in a minimum amount of time. Once you have done this version a few times, you'll discover that you can enter a deeply relaxed state within just a few seconds by closing your eyes and taking a few deep breaths.

Some people find that conscious relaxation of this kind is enhanced by playing very soft, relaxing music in the background. Make sure it remains very peaceful throughout.

Meditation

Deep Relaxation

*F*irst give yourself permission to take five to ten minutes to relax deeply, without having to think about other things you should be doing. Choose a quiet place and time of day when this will be possible.

Loosen any tight clothing.

Sit with your back well supported in a comfortable position, hands gently resting in your lap with your palms open, or lie down on your back with a pillow under your knees if needed.

Take a deep breath and exhale slowly, allowing your shoulders to be loose and relaxed.

Open your mouth wide. Yawn, or pretend you are yawning.Let the areas around your eyes and forehead be relaxed and loose. Let the areas around your nose, mouth, and jaw be relaxed.

Breathe slowly and easily.

If ideas or feelings come into your mind at this time, pretend they are a telephone ringing in the distance, perhaps in a neighbor's house. Acknowledge that "someone is calling," but you do not have to answer.

Take a deep breath, inhaling gently and slowly, imagining the breath entering your right nostril. Hold the breath for a moment, then exhale slowly and comfortably, imagining that you are exhaling through your left nostril.

Take another deep breath, this time imagining your breath entering your left nostril and exiting your right.

Focus your attention on how your breath feels: cooling, as it enters your nostrils, perhaps gently expanding your chest as it fills your lungs, then slightly warming your nostrils as you exhale. You may wish to visualize the air as having a beautiful, vibrant color as it enters and exits your body.

Repeat this breathing pattern until you have done at least four full cycles. A full cycle is one inhalation and one exhalation.

Now with each cycle, focus your attention on one area of your body:

> Be aware of your scalp relaxing.
> Be aware of your eyes, ears, and jaw relaxing.
> Be aware of your neck relaxing.
> Be aware of your shoulders relaxing.
> Be aware of your chest relaxing.
> Be aware of your upper back relaxing.
> Be aware of your arms and hands relaxing.
> Be aware of your abdomen relaxing.
> Be aware of your buttocks relaxing.
> Be aware of your legs relaxing.
> Be aware of your feet relaxing.

Now let your breathing pattern return to normal as you enjoy the relaxed state you have created.

For several weeks, practice this relaxation exercise whenever the opportunity arises or whenever you feel a need to unwind and rest at work, at home, or in your recreational life.

From the book *The Path of Transformation: How Healing Ourselves Can Change the World* by Shakti Gawain.

Contacting Your Inner Guide

*M*ost of us in this day and age and in our Western society lead very hectic lives. We have many responsibilities: our work, our families, our friendships, our social, community, and political responsibilities. Even our recreational activities often take a lot of our attention and energy. We are very involved in what's outside us.

At the same time, I believe that each of us has a deep sense of truth within us, the guiding force that can lead us successfully through our lives. Most of us are greatly in need of balancing our outward focus by taking some time to go within ourselves. We need to get back in contact with our spirit, with our inner creative source.

In addition, most of us have not been educated to believe in that inner intuitive knowingness. We've been taught to follow outside rules, other people's ideas of what's right and wrong for us or what we need to be doing. As a result, we lose touch with the very core of our being.

We need to take some time to cultivate contact with our inner guidance. We need to reeducate ourselves to pay attention to that part of us that really knows. It helps if we can begin to take some regular time for this — even if it's just a few minutes each day or even a few minutes once a week. We need this time to learn to relax our bodies and our minds, to move into the deeper awareness that exists within us.

This takes practice, patience, and support. But it's something that's very natural for us, so as we begin to cultivate this habit we will find it easier and easier to go within. After a while we will begin to find that we crave this inner contact. When we spend too much time looking outward there will be a part of us that will start to pull us inside and demand that we get in contact with our deeper self.

Meditation

Discovering Your Inner Sanctuary

*T*his visualization meditation will help you begin to establish the practice of moving your attention within, finding a place of relaxation and peace and contacting your inner wisdom. Before we begin, I'd like to remind you that any time you are doing a visualization meditation, do it in a way that comes easily and naturally for you. Don't worry if you don't see a visual image when you meditate. Some people are visually oriented; others are more audio or feeling oriented. So if you get just a feeling about it or even if you are only thinking about it, do whatever comes naturally and easily for you. Accept this, and relax and enjoy it. Also, if I give you certain suggestions but what comes to you is something different from what I suggest, trust your own experience. Always go with what feels right for you.

To begin the meditation, get into a comfortable position, either sitting or lying down. If you're sitting, it's good to be sitting with your back straight and well supported in a comfortable chair, with your feet flat on the floor and your hands in a relaxed position. If you prefer to lie down, lie flat on your back in a very comfortable, relaxed position.

When you are comfortable, close your eyes and become aware of your body; just notice how your body is feeling right now.... If you notice any tense places in your body, gently breathe into those places. Imagine them relaxing and all unnecessary tension releasing and dissolving.

First, put your attention on your feet and imagine relaxing them....

Next, put your attention on your ankles and the calves of your legs and gently relax them....

Now put your awareness in your thighs and your hips. Relax the upper part of your legs and your whole pelvic area....

Gently breathe into the lower part of your body and feel it become very relaxed....

Now put your awareness in your abdomen and your stomach, the area of your internal organs, and imagine all your organs relaxing, functioning easily, comfortably, healthfully, and smoothly....

Relax your chest and relax your shoulders, your arms, your hands, and your fingers....

Put your awareness in your neck and throat, and imagine this part of your body relaxing completely. If there's any tension in this area, imagine it flowing down through your arms and out your fingers, out onto the floor and down into the earth....

And now relax your head, your face...relax your scalp...relax your ears and relax your eyelids. Relax your jaw....

Let your awareness scan through your entire body, from head to toe, from toe to head, and feel your entire body deeply relaxed....Imagine that you can feel life energy flowing smoothly and freely through your entire body. If any area feels tight or tense, gently release it and feel that energy flowing through it....

Take a deep breath, and as you exhale, release any last holding that you're doing in your body. Feel your body totally relax....

Take another deep breath, and as you exhale, relax your mind. Pretend that your mind is just another muscle in your body that you can now relax. You don't have to hold on to any thoughts. You can let everything go for right now and let your mind become very quiet and slow, even a little bit out of focus....

Take another deep breath, and as you exhale, move your awareness into a very deep place inside of you....

Now imagine that you are walking down a path in some very beautiful, natural environment. You may either see the environment visually, or you may feel or sense or pretend that it's there. As you walk down the path you feel the beauty of nature around you...and you feel yourself in an increasingly relaxed state of mind....

Imagine that you come to a clearing or some very beautiful spot, and begin to look around or sense or feel what this place is like. It's a very special, magical place. Notice what's there. Are there trees? Are there plants? Is there an ocean or a river? Are you on a mountain or in a field or in a garden? Let your imagination tell you what this place is.... It's very peaceful and beautiful and it's also very private and safe. This is your own personal, inner sanctuary that you are creating for yourself, inside of you. No one can come here unless invited. This is your own private place.

Feel how warm or how cool it is.... Is it sunny or shady or a combination of both? How does the air feel and how does it smell? What kind of sounds are there in your inner sanctuary? Do you hear birds or insects or the breeze blowing through the trees, or the sound of the ocean? Or is it just very quiet? Are there any flowers or animals near you? Take whatever comes to you that feels right and feels good....

Imagine that you are wandering around your inner sanctuary, getting to know it, getting comfortable in it and familiar with it.... Find a place in your sanctuary that feels like a comfortable place to sit or lie down, and make yourself totally at home there.... Feel the beauty and the nurturing quality of nature all around you, and allow yourself to open up and receive that beauty and that nurturing. Imagine that you're like a sponge, simply absorbing and receiving the love and the beauty of Mother Nature....

And now move your awareness into a deep, quiet place inside of you...keep imagining going deeper and deeper inside yourself until you come to a place of rest and peace within, where all the cares of the world seem far away. Take a moment to simply let yourself be in that peaceful place within, where there's absolutely nothing you have to do or even think about or figure out, a state of quiet beingness....

In this deep, quiet, restful place within yourself you are in contact with your own deepest wisdom, your own natural inner knowingness, the part of you that's very wise and knows everything that you need and is able to give you guidance in your life, moment by moment. Even if you don't feel it or don't quite believe it, just allow yourself to pretend or imagine that it is there. Whether or not you feel it or believe it, it is always there within you....

If you have questions you want to ask your inner guide, go ahead and ask.... Quietly be open to receiving, sensing, or feeling what that wisest part of you may have to say in answer to your question. It may come to you in words. It may come to you in an image. Or it may be just a feeling. Take whatever comes, and allow it to enter your awareness.... It's all right if you feel that nothing is coming; it may come to you at a later time; it doesn't always come the moment you ask. So accept whatever your experience is right now....

If you have more questions you want to ask your inner wisdom, do so. You can ask for help, for support, for direction, for love, for clarity — go ahead and ask for whatever you desire or need. . . . Whenever you ask, as soon as you ask, the door will open for you to begin to receive whatever your heart truly desires. So simply assume now that whatever you are asking for is beginning to come to you. It may come in a different way than you expect, but it will come. . . .

When you feel ready, become aware once again of your sanctuary and know that this is a beautiful place you can come to any time you desire. It is within you always. All you have to do is relax, close your eyes, take a few deep breaths, and desire to be there. You can go there any time you want. It will be a place where you can relax and get in touch with that deep, inner wisdom. . . .

For now, say good-bye to your sanctuary and begin to walk up the path. . . . As you walk up the path, become aware of your body in the room. Feel the room around you. . . . When you feel ready, very gently open your eyes and come back feeling relaxed, energized, and deeply connected with yourself.

Meditation

Contacting Your
Wise Being

*T*here are many ways we can learn to tap into the wisdom within us. The previous meditation is one of the simplest and easiest ways to go inside and find that wisdom, that knowingness within.

Another way to tap into your inner wisdom is to allow yourself to make contact with an image of a very wise being who is your adviser, your spirit guide, your helper, your counselor, your guardian angel, whatever you want it to be. For some people it's easiest to do it this way. For many, it's wonderful to have the option of using both meditations, on different days.

This is a meditation to get in contact with the wise being that is a part of you. To do this, go back into your inner sanctuary. And once again remember, whatever you experience is your own way of doing this, whether you visualize, whether you feel, sense, or just think about it.

Take what comes to you easily and trust your own experience as long as it feels right to you.

Find a comfortable place to sit or lie down. Be sure your spine is straight. Get in a position so your body can deeply relax. . . .

Take a deep breath. As you exhale, begin to relax your body. Close your eyes. . . . Take another deep breath, and as you exhale, relax your body a little more. . . . Take another deep breath. As you exhale, imagine relaxing your body as completely as you can. . . . If there are any places in your body that still feel tight or tense — where you're holding energy you don't need — put your awareness into those places, breathe into them, and, as you exhale, imagine the tension or the excess energy releasing and draining away so that your entire body feels deeply relaxed. . . .

Imagine feeling the life force, life energy, flowing freely and easily through your entire body, nourishing every cell of your body, releasing the old that you no longer need and replacing it with new, vital energy and aliveness. . . .

Now take another deep breath, and as you exhale, relax your mind. . . . Let go of any problems, preoccupations, cares, or responsibilities that you have on your mind right now — just for a little while. You can always bring these things back when it's appropriate. But for the next few minutes, let them all go.... Let your mind grow quiet and move slowly.... As thoughts come up in your mind, as they inevitably do, just notice them and then release them. Don't stay focused on the thoughts. Release each thought as soon as you notice it....

Imagine that your mind is becoming very peaceful and quiet, like a still lake or pond, so peaceful there's not even a ripple on the surface....

Take another deep breath, and as you exhale, imagine moving your awareness into a very deep place inside of you.... Then imagine you are walking down that beautiful path in nature, feeling the peace and beauty of nature around you.... As you walk, you gradually feel more and more relaxed and open ... and you come, once again, into your inner sanctuary, which may be a meadow, a mountaintop, a spot in the woods, a cave, or a beach — anywhere you desire it to be....

You may find yourself in the same place as before, or it could be a different place. Let it be however you want it to be. But know that this is a very peaceful, beautiful, and safe place for you to be. It's a very private place. It's yours. No one else can come here unless invited.

Take a few moments just to be and feel and see, to be aware of your sanctuary and how it feels to be there.... Walk around, feel the air, notice the other living beings, the plants or animals or birds....

And then, find a place in your sanctuary to make yourself very comfortable and at home. You can sit down if you wish....

Now look back toward the entrance to your sanctuary, and imagine that you begin to see or sense or feel the presence of a very wise being who is about to enter. This wise being could be a man or a woman, a child or an animal. Or it might be a color or an ethereal presence....

Begin to feel or picture or sense this wise being as it steps through the entrance to your sanctuary and begins to move toward you.... See or feel how old or how young, how big or how small... how this wise being moves, how he or she is dressed if it's a person.... Most importantly, feel the energy of this wise being as it moves toward you....

As it comes closer, greet the wise being in any way that feels appropriate to you.... Trust your own feelings. Allow the wise being to greet you and make contact. You can make contact through words or energetically, telepathically, through touch, or in any way that feels intuitively right. Know that this wise being is here to serve you, to help you in whatever way you need. . . .

The wise being may have a message for you, so ask now if it has something to tell you, in words or in any other way, something to remind you of or to let you know. And then be open to hearing or sensing or feeling what the message is. . . . If there is something you especially need or want, ask for it, whether it be some words of wisdom or some loving support — whatever it may be, go ahead and ask. . . . Let yourself receive the response that this wise being gives to you. . . .

Now continue to be together in whatever way feels good to you. . . . You may wish to be together without words, or you may want to talk. . . . Allow yourself to receive and fully enjoy this experience. And when you feel ready, complete your contact in whatever way you desire for right now. . . .

If you want to keep the wise being with you in the sanctuary, you can do that. If it feels right for the wise being to leave the sanctuary, if you feel complete with your experience for now, then say good-bye and imagine this being moving back up the path and out of the sanctuary. . . . But know that any time you want to, you can come to this sanctuary, you can ask for your wise being to come and be with you here, and you can ask whatever questions you have or ask for whatever support, guidance, love, or contact you need. . . .

Now once again, look around your sanctuary. . . . Remember that this is a place that you can visit any time you want by closing your eyes, taking a few deep breaths, and desiring to be there. . . .

If you want to sleep after doing this meditation, go ahead and let yourself drift into sleep. . . .

If you want to come out of the meditation, say goodbye to your sanctuary for now and begin to move back up the path. Feel yourself more and more alive, energized, and balanced. . . .

Become aware of your body and how it's feeling now, and become aware of the room around you. . . . When you feel ready, very gradually open your eyes and come back into the room. . . .

If you wish to stay longer with this experience, relax even more deeply and stay with it for as long as you desire. . . .

From the audio *Meditations* by Shakti Gawain.

The Male and Female Within

*E*ach of us, whether man or woman, has masculine and feminine aspects to ourselves, male and female energies within us. I believe that one of our most important challenges in life is to recognize and develop both the male and female aspects of ourselves and to bring those energies into balance within our own being.

The idea of male and female energies has been with us for a long time. The Eastern philosophies have always talked about the yin and yang aspects of the universe. Not only does each of us have yin and yang within; everything in the universe is made up of yin and yang, the two polarized energies: the active and receptive, positive and negative, light and dark, masculine and feminine.

In the West, Carl Jung did pioneering, exciting work with his concept of the anima and animus. He explained that men have a feminine side, the anima, and women have a masculine side, the animus, and that most of us have strongly repressed these aspects of ourselves and we must come to terms with them.

I have found that some people have an initial resistance to using the words female and male for aspects of themselves because in our culture we have so many preconceived ideas about what these words mean. There's a great deal of emotional charge associated with them. If you're uncomfortable with these words, feel free to substitute the words yin and yang, active and receptive, or any others that appeal to you.

I have a particular way of looking at the male and female: I think of the feminine or female aspect of ourselves, whether we're men or women, as the intuitive part of us. It's the deepest and wisest guiding force within us, the receptive door within us that allows the higher power of the universe to enter. It is through the inner feminine that we receive the creative power of the universe. Think of it as the receiving end of the channel, in a sense.

The male aspect is action. It's our ability to take action in physical form in the physical world. It's our ability to do things, to speak, to move our bodies. Think of it as the out-flowing end of the channel. The energy comes in through the receptive, feminine door and moves out through the masculine ability to take action.

Those two inner forces working together, the female and the male, form the creative process. When we receive the energy through our inner feminine and we express the energy into the world through our inner male, we create something. For example, an artist may awaken with an inspired idea for a painting, an image that is communicated from his inner female, and immediately pick up his brush and begin painting, an action taken by his inner male. Or a mother may feel sudden concern for her child, a warning coming from her inner female, and run into the other room and pull the child away from a hot stove, an action taken by her inner male. Another example is a businessperson who may have an impulse to contact a certain associate, which would be guidance from the inner female. As a result, he or she would make a call and launch a new project, action taken by the inner male.

An example of how this works in my life is that when I feel moved to write, the initial impulse comes from the higher power of the universe and reaches me through my female, my intuitive feeling in the form of a prompting: "Gee, I'd like to write something. I have something I want to say." Then it's carried out by my masculine self; I get a piece of paper and sit down and write something. And something is created through the union of the male and female within me, through the female initiating the creativity and the male carrying it forth.

Here's a simple way of putting it: The female in us says, "I feel this." The male in us says, "I hear you — what would you like me to do?" She says, "I want that." He says, "You want that? Okay, great. I'll get it for you." This union of feminine and masculine energies within the individual is the basis of all creation. Female intuition plus male action equals creativity.

For us to live a harmonious and creative life, we need to have both energies functioning fully, and working together. It's necessary for us to put the female energy in the guiding position. Her natural function is as our guide. The female energy is tuned in to the higher intelligence of the universe. Naturally we want to be guided by that highest intelligence. The function of the male energy is to listen to that intelligent guidance and to figure out how to carry it out in the world. The true function of male energy is clarity, directness, and a passionate strength based on what the universe inside of us, coming through our female, tells us.

It's important to remember that I'm talking about an internal process. People sometimes become confused and upset because they externalize what I'm saying. They think I'm saying that women should tell men what to do, that men should listen to women for their guidance, that men should do everything for women.

That's not what I'm saying — I'm saying that within each of us, the feminine aspect of our being, which is the inner guidance, needs to be the initiating energy, and the masculine aspect is the energy that carries out our inner knowingness.

The idea of male and female is really just another way of saying that we need to listen to our own truth, our own knowingness, and be willing to act on it.

When we take the concepts of male and female energies and project them externally, we become confused. A lot of the stereotyped ideas of feminine and masculine energies really apply to how they're meant to function internally, but we have tried to make them function externally by saying women are supposed to be this way and men are supposed to be that way. And then we limit ourselves: women play out only the feminine energy and men play out only the male energy. We need to have both. Internally, each individual is a complete male/female being.

Sometimes people feel afraid when they hear about this idea. They fear we're all going to end up alike. If we're complete masculine/feminine beings, we're all going to be androgenous. I haven't found that to be true. What I find to be true is that when a woman allows her male energy to support her internally, when she starts trusting that male energy, she feels safer to become more feminine, to become more open, softer, more emotional, more receptive, knowing her masculine strength will support and take care of her. Likewise, when men allow themselves to feel the power of their feminine, it enhances their masculinity. They feel energetic, stronger, they feel more powerful.

Rather than becoming androgenous, more alike, our masculinity or femininity becomes enhanced so that we can play the outside game however we want to, without limiting ourselves by being stuck only in one-half our being.

Most of us have not yet learned how to allow our male and female energies to function naturally in the proper relationship with each other. In our culture, we've used our male energy, our ability to think and act, to suppress and control our feminine intuition rather than to support and express her. This traditional patriarchal use of the male energy I call the "old male." It exists equally in men and women, although it is often more obvious and external in men and more subtle and internal in women. The old male is that part of us that wants to keep control. War is a good example of the old male energy lacking the wisdom and direction of the female. He's terrified of feminine power because he doesn't want to surrender to the power of the universe. He's afraid that if he surrenders he will lose his individual identity.

In relationship with the old male, the female is helpless in the world. Her power can't move directly into the world. So it often comes out in indirect ways.

If we cannot express our female energy through our male energy, then it can come out only indirectly, covertly through manipulation. The energy has to go somewhere; if it doesn't come out directly, it can cause problems for us, even physical illness.

The old male part of us is afraid of the power of the feminine because it's the power of spirit. It's the power of the universe and it feels like it's going to be totally out of control. And we're afraid to let go of that control. We're afraid to surrender to the power of the universe and trust that the higher power really does know what to do.

In a sense, the old male is afraid that the power of the female is greater than he is. And in some ways that may be true, but what will counteract this fear is that the more the male within us begins to listen to the female and take action, physical action, the more his strength is increased. He becomes more and more empowered from the power of the female. Eventually we can have physical bodies so flexible and so powerful that we can handle more and more of the universal creative energy coming through us.

The more our male aspect listens to our female aspect and acts on her guidance, the stronger our channel becomes, the more creative energy can flow through it, and the more our bodies can handle it. So we build our strength, we build our clarity, we build our channel every time we listen to our intuitive prompting and take the risk, have the courage to act on it in every way in our lives, the small things as well as the large.

The small things, in fact, are the most important. For example, when we feel as if we want to say something but we don't say it because we're afraid somebody may not like it, the male in us is failing to carry out the prompting of our inner female. If we can reverse that, even once or twice, it makes a big difference. When you feel you want to say something and you have the courage to go ahead and say it, you feel an empowerment. That feeling is your male aspect listening to your female. When somebody invites you to go somewhere and you don't really want to go, but you do it because you *should*, that is an example of the old male carrying out an action for a reason other than the prompting of the female. But if you feel you don't want to go and your male supports that by saying, "No, I don't want to do that right now," you'll become a little more empowered from that action of trusting yourself.

As men and women, we have played out these old male and female energies in our traditional roles. The traditional role of the male is to be very strong, in control, to cut off his feelings, to be almost like a machine, unemotional, and, in fact, suppressive toward women. That's because internally he's suppressing his own inner female.

The traditional macho man has a helpless, hysterical female voice inside of him desperately trying to be heard. He will tend to attract women who have low self-esteem and are clingy and needy, or who express their power indirectly through manipulation: little girl cuteness, sexual seductiveness, cattiness, or dishonesty.

The traditional role of a woman has been to be emotional and intuitive, but not to be able to empower herself to translate that into action in the world. Therefore, she becomes manipulative; she can't exercise her power directly, so she must exercise it indirectly. She feels helpless and dependent on men.

From this perspective, each person is only half a person, dependent on the other half for his or her very existence. But because we cannot live healthy lives in the world without the full range of masculine and feminine energies, each sex has been helplessly dependent on the other for survival. In some ways it may seem like a perfectly workable arrangement. Men help women, women help men. But there is one underlying problem: as an individual, if you don't feel whole, if you feel your survival depends on another person, you are constantly afraid of losing that person. But you know on a deep level that the person you're attracted to is a mirror of yourself. You must not be too dependent on him or her because you know that everything you see in your partner is also in you. You recognize that the reason you're in the relationship is to learn about yourself and deepen your connection with the universe.

I believe that every form of intimate relationship represents each being's attempt to find its feminine and masculine balance within, from the most traditional marriage to open or homosexual or bisexual relationships. I believe that by finding the balance of the male and female within each of us as individuals, we can relate to another person from a place of wholeness: "I am a complete male/female human being and you are mirroring that completion in me. You are mirroring that wholeness in me." And by reflecting each other we can learn from each other.

Many women like myself have had a strongly developed male energy but have used it in the old male way. I was very intellectual, very active, and drove myself very hard to shoulder the responsibilities of the world. I also had a very strongly developed female, but I didn't put her in charge. In fact, I often ignored her. I basically protected my sensitive, vulnerable feelings by erecting a tough outer shell. I've had to learn to take that powerful male energy and use it to listen to, trust, and support my female. This allows her the safety and support to emerge fully. I feel and appear softer, more receptive, and more vulnerable, but now I'm really much stronger.

Women are now learning to validate themselves instead of abandoning their responsibility and getting a man to do it for them. However, they are challenging a deep-seated pattern that has endured for centuries, and it takes time to change it in the deepest layers of our psyche. The key is to keep listening to, trusting, and acting on our deepest feelings.

The union of the male and female within each person allows true love and true passion to come from the universe through each of us. Our relationships can then be based on the love and the passion of the universe rather than on a feeling of inadequacy.

The feminine power, the power of spirit, is always within us. It's up to our male energy to determine how we relate to that power. We can either fight it, block it, and attempt to control it and keep ourselves separate from it, or we can surrender and open to it, trust it, support it, and move with it.

As each of us deals with this individually, we also deal with it collectively in our culture and in our world.

I believe that the world is moving from a position of fear and distrust of the female power by the male energy within us to a position of trusting and supporting that power of spirit by the new male within us, being willing to bring that spirit through and express it in the world. As each of us makes that transformation, we see our individual lives beginning to come into balance and harmony. Our relationships begin to reflect that harmony, and eventually the entire world begins to transform and reflect that.

The power of the feminine energy is on the rise in our world. As she emerges within us and we acknowledge and surrender to her, the old male within us is transformed. He re-emerges, reborn through the female as the new male, the one who goes all out in his trust and love for her. He must grow to become her equal in power so that they can be the lovers they are meant to be.

I believe the new male has truly been born in our consciousness only within the last few years. Before that we had very little experience in our bodies of the true male energy. Our only concept of the male was the old male. The birth of the new male is synonymous with the birth of the new age. The new world is being built within us and mirrored around us as the new male emerges in all its glory from the feminine power of the spirit.

Meditation

Contacting Your
Male and Female

*L*et's take a moment now to contact our male
and female aspects.

Find a comfortable position, sitting straight with your
back well supported, or lying down comfortably, flat
on your back.... Close your eyes. Take a deep breath,
and as you exhale, relax your body.... Take another
deep breath, and as you exhale, relax your body
more.... Take another deep breath, and as you exhale,
see if you can relax every part of your body.... If there
are any areas of your body that still feel tension, put
your awareness into those areas. Breathe into them
and gently release.... Continue to breathe deeply and

naturally, and imagine that you can feel the flow of energy all the way through your body, from your toes to the tips of your fingers to the top of your head. . . .

Take another deep breath, and as you exhale, relax your mind. . . . Let each thought that comes into your mind gently float away and allow your mind to slow and come into a soft focus. . . . Take another deep breath, and as you exhale, allow your awareness to move into a very deep, quiet place inside. . . .

Imagine that you are walking down a path in a beautiful place in nature, and as you walk down the path you feel yourself becoming more and more centered, calm, and relaxed. . . . You come to a beautiful place, your inner sanctuary. . . you enter the sanctuary. . . . Take a few moments to feel, see, or experience that beautiful place that is your own private, personal, inner sanctuary. . . . It is very safe and quiet, a place you can visit to feel nurtured and to find quiet time with yourself. . . . Notice what's in your sanctuary: the plants or trees, the water, if there's sun or shade, how warm or how cool it is. . . . Then find a place in your sanctuary to sit down and be very comfortable. . . .

Today you're going to bring into your sanctuary images of your male and female selves. Imagine that you look toward the entrance to the sanctuary, and coming down the path, you see or sense a female figure.... It could be a woman, a girl, an animal, or it could be a color or a shape or energy. As she approaches the entrance to the sanctuary, see or feel what she looks like, how old or young she is, and how she's dressed.... Notice how she moves....

As she comes closer, you begin to feel her energy field. Notice what her energy feels like.... She comes near to you now and you greet each other.... She has a message she wants to communicate to you. Ask her what she needs to say to you or to communicate to you, whether it be in words or some other form, and then receive whatever you feel her message is.... Ask her what she needs or wants from you, either now or in your life in general....

She has a gift to give you. Allow yourself now to receive her gift....

Spend a little time being with her in whatever way feels right for both of you.... As you're with her, allow yourself to really feel her energy and imagine that you could bring her energy inside of you and experience it in your body. What does her energy feel like in your body?

Then release her energy from your body and complete your interaction with her for right now in whatever way feels good to you.... Ask her if she will stay near you. Perhaps she would like to sit or stand on your left side, whatever feels best for her and for you....

Once again look toward the entrance to your sanctuary and become aware that coming down the path is the figure, the image, or the sense of a male form.... This could be a man, a boy, an animal, a color, or shape. Begin to see or sense that this is the representation of your inner male energy at this time. As he moves into the sanctuary and comes a little closer, notice more details about what he looks like, how he moves, how he's dressed.... Begin to feel and sense his energy.... As he moves closer, feel his energy more strongly as you see and sense him more clearly....

When he comes close to you, greet each other. He also has a message for you. It may be in words, or it may be communicated in some other way, either telepathically or through actions. Ask him to give you his message...and just trust what comes to you.... Ask him what he needs from you, either right at this moment or in general in your life....

He, too, has a gift to give you. Allow yourself to receive his gift....

Feel his energy and imagine that you can bring his energy into your body for a moment. Let yourself feel what it feels like to have his energy in your body.... Then release his energy from your body and complete your interaction with him for the moment in whatever way feels right....

Now allow your male and female selves to meet each other, to greet each other in whatever way they desire.... Ask them if they have something they want to say to each other or communicate to each other in words or in any other way.... Ask them if they have anything they need from each other....

Imagine that you can feel both of their energies or each of their energies separately.... Imagine that you can bring both energies into your body for a moment.... Feel the balance, or the contrast.... Then release their energies and allow them to complete their interaction with each other and with you in whatever way feels intuitively right....

When you feel complete with this experience, either ask them to stay with you in the sanctuary for awhile, for however long feels right for all of you, or imagine them moving back up the path and out of the sanctuary, knowing that you can always bring them back whenever you want to, just by wishing for them to come.... You can always ask them for advice or help, or ask them to express to you anything that you need to know....

If you want to stay in your sanctuary, stay as long as you desire. If you are ready to leave, begin to move back up the path, and as you walk up the path, feel yourself in a state of balance, centeredness, and vitality.... Become aware of your body and of the room around you, and when you feel ready, open your eyes and come back into the room.

From the audio *Meditations* by Shakti Gawain.

Discovering Your Inner Child

*M*ost of us think we're supposed to be one consistent personality, and we wonder why we sometimes feel so inconsistent. One day we feel one way, another day we feel another way. Sometimes one minute we feel one way and the next minute we feel a different way. What I've been discovering is that we're not one person at all. We all have many people inside us, many different characters.

Think of these people as being different sub-personalities. Each is distinctly its own character, with its own set of needs and desires, its own point of view, its own opinions. Often these sub-personalities are diametrically opposed to one another. We have a part of us, for example, that thinks the most important thing to do is work very hard and become successful.

And if that part of us were running the show we would be working all the time. On the other hand, there may also be a part completely opposite who just wants to relax, hang out, goof off, and enjoy life.

Usually, we're more identified with one or the other of these parts within. If we're a workaholic type of person, we are heavily identified with the character in us that's a hard worker, and we generally ignore, deny, or suppress the other character in us that's perhaps the hedonist, the pleasure lover, or the one that likes to simply *be*. Sometimes we feel the conflict between the two and we bounce back and forth between them.

It's very interesting to get to know all the people inside and to respect them all. Each of them, in fact, is an important part of us. Each is an aspect of our personality that we need to learn to know, respect, explore, and appreciate. By allowing ourselves to know and express *all* the sub-personalities within us, we can become balanced instead of being identified with only one side of a polarity. Ideally, we want to explore both sides of the polarity and then be able to choose the appropriate moments for the different sub-personalities to run the show.

Coming to know all your selves is quite a fascinating exploration. I sometimes think of myself as being a family, not just one person. And as in most families, there's a certain amount of conflict, and there's also a lot of love. The idea is to let every member of the inner family play its role, express itself, and be respected for the part that it plays in the family, so that ultimately the family can be in harmony.

Another interesting metaphor for this situation inside of you is to think of yourself as being a committee. When you think about yourself as a committee, it often explains why it is so difficult for you to get a job done or make a decision. We all know what happens when a decision is made by a committee. One person wants one thing, another wants another, and half the time nothing gets done. If you can get to know the members of your inner committee and allow them to express themselves clearly, then *you,* as a conscious person, can begin to make the decisions, instead of allowing whichever part of you happens to grab control in any given moment make the decisions.

Another way I like to look at this is to think of myself as a theater, and all the characters are playing out their dramas on an inner stage. We tend to attract people into our lives who reflect the various characters inside ourselves — we are attracted to people, and attract people to us, who are similar to our sub-personalities. In this way we play out the inner drama externally. Many lessons in our lives involve learning to see the reflections of people in our lives and what they show us about our inner selves.

The ultimate point is to come to know, love, and accept all aspects of ourselves. There's no part of us that's bad. Everything in the universe wants to be loved and wants to be accepted. Whatever you're not loving and not accepting will follow you around until you love and accept it.

For many of us, for example, it's difficult to accept that there's a person in us that's angry. In fact, it's *really* angry because it's never been listened to and hasn't had a chance to be accepted. But when you can start to find safe, comfortable, appropriate ways to allow your anger to be felt and experienced and expressed appropriately, that self eventually becomes an accepted part of you, and a lot of the "charge" dissolves.

Each inner character is very important in our lives, and each has gifts to give us. But one of the most important parts of ourselves is our inner child, the child that lives inside each of us always. In fact, we have many children within ourselves. We have within a child of every age, from earliest infancy through adolescence.

These children within have many different aspects. We have a child within that is very vulnerable, very emotional. In fact, the child inside of us is the seat of our emotions. So, to learn to be in contact with our emotions and to love and accept our feelings, we must be in touch with the vulnerable child within us.

There is a child in us that's very playful, that knows how to have fun, just as little children naturally know how to have a good time, know how to play. We all have that child within us, a child that naturally sparkles and has fun and plays and is constantly looking for what's fun in life.

We also have a magical child inside us. This is the part that is naturally tuned in to the magic of the universe. As adults, most of us have forgotten about this magic. When we were children we knew there was magic and we were connected with that magic. We naturally understood the magic of little plants and animals, and maybe we were even in contact with elves and fairies or whatever magic meant to us.

There's also a very wise child within us. It's a part of us that's very truthful, that sees and knows what we're feeling, what other people are feeling, that has the power to cut through much of the superficial dishonesty that exists in adult society, and always goes right to the core truth of situations.

A good way to start to get in touch with or become aware of the child (or many other sub-personalities) within us is to look at real children. Children reflect the child inside us. I'm sure you've all had experiences when you've looked into an infant's eyes and felt a very profound connection. Or you've seen a child be very playful, and it brings out that playful part of you. Or you've had a child say something to you that's so profoundly wise you feel extremely moved by it. You feel that this child in a way knows more than you do. That's a reflection of the knowing-ness of your inner child.

The child within us is certainly one of the most important aspects of ourselves to contact. One reason is that, as spiritual beings, we come into a physical body and are born into this world as a child, as an infant. So the child is the closest part of our personality to the spiritual essence. When the child is born it is almost purely spiritual essence, because at that point it has no contact or experience with the world. That is why we are so moved when we are with very young children; we see the reflection of our own profound and beautiful and innocent spiritual essence. In the child, this essence has not yet been buried or hidden.

As we get in touch with the child inside us, we get in touch with our deepest and purest spiritual essence. By cultivating the relationship with the inner child, we automatically form a deeper and stronger connection with our essence, and our spiritual essence can then come through.

Another important reason for getting in touch with our inner child is that the child is the key to our creativity. We all know how creative children are, unless they've already been inhibited. Very young children are endlessly creative. They're always playing some kind of game of imagination so easily. You know: Let's play house. Let's play fireman. Let's pretend this. Let's pretend that. And they go right into that imaginary world.

They're filled with imagination and creativity. They love to draw. They love to paint. They're always singing little songs. They dance. They're magically creative beings.

All of us are that way, too. We all had that magical, creative essence within us as children, but as adults we have suppressed it, we have inhibited it. So, as we get in touch with the child inside us, we release our creativity.

The key to creativity is being willing to try something, to risk doing it and seeing what happens. Our creative child is the part of us that's not afraid to try new things. When children draw pictures, they don't worry about whether they're going to look exactly the way some critic thinks they should look. They just do it for the joy of it. And that's how our creative energy can be freed, by feeling the essence of that child within us and being willing to try things that are fun and enjoyable and exciting and new and different. I find over and over again that as people get in touch with the child, they open whole new areas of creativity within themselves, which is immensely fun and rewarding.

Also the child is the key to intimacy in relationships. Because the child is the part of us that feels the deepest emotions, it's the part of us that can truly love. And it's also the part of us that's vulnerable, the part that can be wounded, hurt. To feel real intimacy with another person you must be in touch with your vulnerability, with your love, even with your ability to be wounded.

So, it's the vulnerable child within us that allows us to feel intimacy and closeness with other people. If we are not in touch with our child, we will not experience true intimacy. As we learn to be in touch with the child and take care of the child and protect and express the child in appropriate ways, we can experience intimacy in healthy, fulfilling ways in our lives.

Some people are in touch with their inner child. Perhaps some of you already know that you are in touch with your child or you may know people who are in touch with their child. These people are usually fun to be around or move us emotionally. They touch us as a child does.

But most of us have suppressed or buried the child because at a very young age we discovered that it's not a very safe world for the child. So, from the very earliest times in our lives we began to build defenses and protection for the child. Most of our personality structure, in fact, is a defense, created to take care of that very sensitive, vulnerable, feeling essence that is the inner child. We build stronger and stronger walls of defense, more and more mechanisms for surviving in a tough world that's not set up for this innocent child.

Eventually, the child that we're trying to protect gets totally buried inside us, and we don't even know it exists. That's the predicament most of us are in. We automatically run on our defense systems and our survival mechanisms, and we forget that the reason we have them is to take care of and fulfill the needs of the child. But the child inside us is in pain because its needs are not being met. The child does not go away. It never grows up. It never dies. It is with us through our entire lives.

If we're not conscious of those needs, then we are constantly trying to fulfill them unconsciously. The child within is unconsciously motivating all our behavior. We may, for example, develop a sub-personality that's a workaholic because it's trying to make enough money to make the child feel safe and protected. But we end up forgetting about the child and spend our whole lives working hard. We may accumulate a lot of money and a lot of success, but none of it gives us the satisfaction we need because we've forgotten about the child who was the original motivating force.

Sometimes the child will actually sabotage our attempts to be successful or do the things we think we should do, because secretly the child knows that its needs are not going to be met by what we're striving for. I've found that when people have a block about being successful in life, often the block comes from the inner child whose needs are not being met. The child will stop you from being successful until you start to give it more nurturing, more love, more time to play, or whatever it needs.

So our challenge is to get in touch with the inner child, to find out what the child's needs are, and to begin consciously to take care of the child. The child's needs are for love, for physical and emotional contact, for enjoyment, and to express itself honestly and creatively. As we begin to find ways of meeting those needs, we find our whole personality starts to come into alignment, and we become healthy and balanced.

There are many ways to get in touch with the child inside us: through playing, dancing, singing, drawing, painting, by being in nature, or by hanging out with children and allowing ourselves to experience our inner child. Buy a toy or a stuffed animal, and allow your inner child to express what it wants and needs in ways that are fun. Often the child inside comes forth with animals, because children naturally love animals.

One way that's been very helpful for many people is through the meditation that follows.

Meditation

Contacting Your Inner Child

*B*efore starting this meditation, be sure you create the most positive possible environment for the safety and comfort of the child. Find a place that feels very comfortable and private. You may want to have a blanket, a stuffed animal, or something else that will make your child feel welcome. You may want to meditate outdoors in a special place or find a special place in your house that feels nurturing to you.

When you first do this meditation, it's important to keep a few things in mind. Sometimes, even though we have spent most of our lives not being in touch with our inner child, our first attempt will be very easy. The child has been waiting for us and wanting that contact with us. But sometimes the child is not yet ready to trust us, so it may take a little patience. The child may hold back until it knows that you really want this contact and that you're willing to be responsible and consistent with the contact.

When you first do this meditation, trust what comes, trust what happens. If the child is a little reserved or a little hesitant, just give the child time. Keep doing the meditation regularly and you'll find that the contact will continue to increase and become stronger and more positive. For now, though, simply accept whatever happens.

It may be that you'll get in touch with a child who's very emotional, sad, or hurt. Or, you may get in touch with a child who's very playful and wants to be with you and have fun. You may be in touch with the magical aspect of your child, or with the wise child. Accept what comes to you, because that will be the part that's ready to be discovered at this time. As you continue to work with this meditation, you may discover different aspects of the child. Trust your own experience.

Get comfortable, either sitting or lying down. If you're sitting up, be sure your back is supported so you can sit straight. If you're lying down, lie down comfortably, flat on your back. Close your eyes.... Take a deep breath, and as you exhale, relax your body.... Take another deep breath, and as you exhale, relax your body deeper and deeper....Take another deep breath, and as you exhale, imagine relaxing your body as completely as you can. Your whole body is now completely relaxed....

Take another deep breath, and as you exhale, relax your mind....Let your thoughts float away; let your mind come into stillness and quiet....Take another deep breath, and as you exhale, imagine moving your awareness into a deep, quiet place inside of you....

Then imagine that you're walking down that beautiful path to your inner sanctuary....And as you walk down the path, you feel more and more relaxed, centered, and comfortable. You enter your sanctuary and sense and feel the beauty and comfort of nature all around you....

Take a few moments to get in touch with your sanctuary, to remember some of the details about this place, and to let yourself enjoy being there....Imagine that you're walking around your sanctuary noticing the various plants and animals, feeling the sun or the breeze, and a little way off in the distance, across the sanctuary, you become aware of the presence of a small child....As you start to move toward the child, you see or sense whether it's a boy or girl, about how old it is, and what the child is doing....

Slowly move toward the child, and as you get closer, notice how the child is dressed.... Allow yourself to sense how the child is feeling emotionally.... Approach the child and make contact in whatever way you sense would be appropriate right now....

Ask the child if there is anything it wants to tell you or wants to communicate to you. It may be in words or it may be in some other way. Allow yourself to receive whatever the child wants to communicate....

Now ask the child what it needs most from you, right now or in your life in general.... Listen to what the child has to tell you, whether in words or in other ways....

Spend a little time being with your child.... Allow the child to guide you in the appropriate way to be with it, whether playing together or simply sitting close or holding each other....

The child has a special gift to give you. Allow yourself now to receive the gift the child has for you....

Continue to be with your child.... Let the child know that you want to be in contact with it as much as you can from now on....

Complete your time together for right now in whatever way feels good for both of you. You and the child have a choice to make. The child can choose to remain there in the sanctuary, in a very safe place inside of you, and you can come to visit the child in your sanctuary. Or, the child can come with you when you leave the sanctuary. Your child will know which way feels best for right now, and it can always change in the future.

If the child is going to stay in the sanctuary, say good-bye for now. Let the child know that you will come back as often as you can, and that you want to know how the child feels and what it needs from you in your life. . . .

If the child is coming with you, take it in your arms or by the hand and start to walk up the path out of the sanctuary. As you walk up the path, feel yourself alive, filled with energy, balanced, and centered. . . .

Become aware of your body in the room, and when you feel ready, open your eyes and come back into the room.

Now that you've gotten in touch with your inner child, it's important to follow through and be consistent in taking care of and being present with this child on a regular basis. You are the parent to your own inner child. It's important to become a conscious, loving, responsible parent to that child. This can be enjoyable for you and for the child, but it also requires some awareness and responsibility on your part. It means that you need to start making some space in your life for that child at appropriate times.

If you're not sure what the needs of your child are or how to best take care of your child, simply ask. The child knows what it wants and what it needs at all times, so cultivate the habit of communicating with the child, asking what it needs, what it wants. Then do your best to give that child the fulfillment of its needs. You can't always do everything the child wants when it wants, but you should include its needs in your life, just as you would with a real child. Make them as much a priority as you can, and you will find that the rewards are great.

Start to think about things that are fun or that are nurturing for the child, and begin to include them in your life in a regular way. Every day, or at least every couple of days, take some time, even if it's just a few minutes in the morning or a few minutes in the evening, and find out what your child likes to do. Get toys the child likes to play with, go for walks, ride a bike, take hot bubble baths, get story books — things that really feed and nurture your inner child. Of course, the most important thing to the child is love and intimacy, so your child will guide you in finding more contact, closeness, friendship, and love with other people.

It's also important to learn when it's not appropriate to bring your child out. The middle of a business meeting at work is probably not the best time to have your child come out. You can allow your child to stay home and play. Just tell the child that you're going off to work and that you'll be home later on, and that you'll take some time to play then.

Even though these things may feel a little silly at first, they will end up bringing much more balance, harmony, enjoyment, and fulfillment into your life.

From the audio *Meditations* by Shakti Gawain.

Expressing
Your Creativity

*M*any people think they're not creative. I hear this all the time in my workshops; people say to me, "I'm not creative." I don't believe it. I've found from working with many people that, after we get through our limited ideas and our blocks and our fears, we are all creative beings. I don't know what more proof we need of our creativity than to look at our lives and realize that, on a metaphysical level, we have created them. Granted, they're not perfect, but they are nevertheless a powerful manifestation of our creativity. We need to acknowledge how incredible our lives really are and therefore how incredible we are. We have all created an enormous amount of powerful, interesting, even amazing experiences and people in our lives. And those are all mirrors of our creativity.

We create our own reality every moment, whether or not we're conscious of it. If we're not conscious, we create it out of habit and old patterns. As we become more and more conscious, we are more able to create what we truly desire.

I find that the idea that we are not creative usually comes from some type of early programming or conditioning that we've received. Somebody along the way told us we weren't creative, and we believed it. Or maybe we got so much criticism or disapproval or not enough encouragement and support to express our natural creativity, that we came to the conclusion that we weren't creative.

Many people tend to equate creativity with only certain types of expression. We all know that art or dance or music are creative, for example, but we don't necessarily think that running a business is creative, or running a home is creative, or that being a parent is creative. And yet, when you think about it, what could be more creative than raising children? That is the ultimate creative act. To create another human being and to learn how to support that human being in expressing his or her creativity is probably the ultimate challenge. Cooking is creative. Many of our recreational activities, and even the little things that we do all the time, are very creative. But because they come easily to us and they're natural, we don't usually think of them as being creative.

Start to think about the things you do that are enjoyable, that come naturally and easily to you, and see
the creative aspect of those expressions, see how those
are a truly important expression of your being. Try
taking some risks. Do some new and different things
that you find creative. I've noticed that a lot of people
have the concept that they're too old to try something
new, especially something "creative" — if they didn't
start it when they were children or very young people,
they figure it's too late to do it now.

I always encourage people to fantasize, to think
about creative things they would like to do. See if
there is something you can do, a step you can take in
the direction of those fantasies, even if they seem a bit
far-fetched. It's never too late.

We know that each of us is in essence a creative
being, a spiritual being who comes into a physical
form. That physical form is our first act of creation.
We create a body to express our spirit. I know that a
lot of us don't like our bodies and don't think they're
the best creation we could have made, but our bodies,
in fact, are in a constant state of creative change. As
we are changing internally, our bodies, as the expression of our spirit, are also changing. So the more you
come to know, acknowledge, and express your creative
spirit, the more your spirit shows in your primary creative project — your body.

Start to look at your body as your creation and see

how it expresses your spirit. Observe the ways that you block yourself from expressing your spirit and see how that is reflected in your body. As you remove these blocks to your creative expression, your body will reflect that transformation.

As adults, the major block to our creativity is our inner critic, that part of us that internally criticizes what we do. We have standards of perfection incorporated from the world around us, ways that we think things *should* be done. We have a critic within who criticizes us when we are not doing things the way the critic feel they should be done. For most of us, this inner critic is what stops us from taking the kinds of risks that need to be taken to be creative.

Creativity requires experimentation. The fundamental principle of creativity is that you do something, you express something, you *try* something. And you must be willing to allow things to be expressed that are not particularly wonderful or perfect or just the way you think they should be expressed. You have to let the expressions flow. People who are creative are willing to make mistakes. Almost all successful persons say that they have had more failures than they've had successes. They have tried many things that have not always worked for them. Some have been very disappointing, but they have continued to take risks and try again.

What stops us from being successful is the critic inside that says, "You're not very smart," "You're not very talented," "You don't know how to do this right," "You're not as good as so-and-so," "You're not as good as you should be," or "Look at what you did, that's not any good," "That's ridiculous," "That's inadequate." We all have, to some degree, that self-criticism. Those of us who have allowed our creativity to flow in our lives have managed in one way or another to set our critic aside long enough to let the energy come through spontaneously.

Dealing with the inner critic is difficult; there's no simple solution. The first step is to recognize your internal critic, to begin to notice what it says to you, and to begin to get in touch with where the voice comes from. For most of us, it began very early in our lives when we were children, when we received criticism from our parents or our siblings or our teachers or those around us, who said, "You don't do that well enough," or "You didn't do that right," or "You're a bad boy or girl," and we've incorporated that criticism. Beginning to become aware of your inner critic, to acknowledge it and notice where it comes from, can start to free you from automatically believing it.

It doesn't seem to help very much simply to try to make the critic shut up. The critic is a strong voice inside us. The key is to begin to notice it and to think to yourself, "Now, do I need to believe this?" "Is this really true?" "Do I have to let this run my life?" "Do I have to let this stop me?"

By asking these questions you can eventually get to a place where you listen to the critic, you acknowledge what it has to say, and then you go ahead and do what you want to do anyway. You could say to yourself "Okay, critic, thank you for sharing your point of view. Now I'm going to go ahead and do this, and even if it isn't perfect, I'm going to do it anyway because I think it'll be fun, or because I want to try something new and I'm willing to let myself be like a child. I'm willing to play, try something and risk and experiment and learn in the process. If I don't do it perfectly, fine; I'll do it again and I'll do it better next time. Or I'll forget it and do something else. It doesn't really matter."

Creativity requires play. It requires fun. It requires a sense of adventure. Learn to look at things a little more lightly and not take them so seriously. If we take ourselves too seriously, we can't have that adventurousness that allows us to explore in new places.

One good way to deal with the critic and begin to free more of your creativity is by using some clearing processes. If you have a journal or if you want to start a journal, try writing your creative voice and then writing any blocks or inhibitions you have about that creative voice. Or try writing the voice of your critic. Write it all down so you can see objectively what it is that stops you, what concepts of yourself you have that stop you from being able to be creative.

Here's a suggestion for starting the flow of your

creativity, getting in touch with how you block yourself, and being able to start to clear some of those
blocks. Think of something you've always wanted to
do that you think of as creative, something you've
never tried or that you've never thought you could do.
For example, if you don't consider yourself an artist,
think about drawing a picture.

Get your materials together: paper, pencils, or
whatever you're going to use for your drawing. Tune
into whatever feelings you have inside that are stop-
ping you, that are telling you you can't draw or that
you won't be able to do it well enough. Then take a
piece of paper and a pen or pencil and write down all
the self-critical or doubting voices or feelings you have
inside. For example: "I'm going to waste this paper
because I'm such a terrible artist," or "I just don't
know how to do this," or "It's going to look really stu-
pid." Write down whatever you are feeling.

Then allow your more creative voice to express itself, and write down what it tells you. It may be something like, "Well, it doesn't really matter how well I do
this, I just want to do it because it'll be fun," or "I just
want to try taking these colors and putting them on
this paper to see what it looks like," or "I just want to
experiment with this." Keep that dialogue going for a
little while until you feel you've cleared enough of
a space to try drawing. Then go ahead and draw.

Carry on the same sort of dialogue until you clear

the space enough so you can feel that you're enjoying what you're doing. It doesn't matter what the result is. The purpose of your creative energy is for your own enjoyment. It's to feel the feeling of being a channel and to allow that creative force to come through you. That is very pleasurable in itself. If you keep that focus in everything you do, you will begin to de-emphasize the necessity for doing things perfectly or producing an exact result — and you will begin to get the same kind of pleasure out of life that children do when they are spontaneously moving with their energy and doing what they feel.

Many people are creative in one area of their lives but not in other areas. If you have one area in which you're creative, you have an advantage in that you know what it's like to allow that creative channel to flow. Think about whatever it is you do in that aspect of your life. If you play music or you are creative in business, what is it that allows you to be creative? How do you get your critic out of the way? How do you trust yourself and express yourself? Think about how you can take the same method you use in your creative area and apply it in other areas of your life, how you can apply it with something new or different so that you allow your creativity to flow in a new direction.

One of the most important aspects of getting in touch with creativity is your fantasies, dreams, and visions. Some people come to workshops and say to me,

"Oh, I don't have any fantasies or visions." But I find, after questioning, that *everybody* has fantasies and dreams and visions. The reason some people think they don't is because they invalidate them. They think, "Oh well, that's nothing," or "That's so foolish it isn't even worth thinking about." Or the fantasies are unconscious and people don't realize they're having them.

Everybody has fantasies about what they want to do, about what they love to do, about what they would do if only they could. So, give yourself a chance to fantasize freely. Enjoy it! If you could have all the money in the world, what would you like to do? If you could do anything you wanted to do, what would it be? Also ask yourself: What kinds of things do I love doing? What comes easily to me? What's fun? What do I do so naturally that I don't even think about it? How could I expand it? How could I possibly make a living from doing the things that I think are the most enjoyable and the most fun? Try not to limit yourself. Be open to all kinds of possibilities that you've never allowed yourself to imagine before.

Some of our fantasies, of course, turn out to be impractical. But I've found that for the most part, the recurring fantasies and dreams we have in our lives contain a great deal of truth. They show us something important about our creative selves: what our purposes are in our lives, what we came here to do, what we want to express. Give yourself a chance to explore and express those fantasies, in your own mind, through writing, through drawing, through talking to a friend, through visualizing. And then ask yourself, "What are some very small, simple steps I can take toward realizing those fantasies?" Even though you may not see how you can pursue your fantasies, ask yourself if there's some simple step you can take in their direction. And then, go ahead; take a risk and do it. See what happens. If it doesn't work out, that's fine. Try something else. Chances are you will discover a whole new creative aspect of your life.

As you start to express your creativity in new ways, don't aim too high and get discouraged. Start with small things. Let yourself take a step that's fun and relatively easy and enjoyable, and then appreciate yourself for that. If you keep taking small steps, you will end up being exactly where you need to be. For example, after you finish reading this section, try thinking of one thing that you can do in your life, today or tomorrow, that would express your creativity in a way that you wouldn't normally consider. You could rearrange your room, for example, in a way that makes your environment a little more creative. Or you could look in your closet and put on the clothes that feel like they would express you in a new and different way today. Or make some other small change in your life.

Then continue looking for little ways to express yourself more creatively and differently. Have fun with it. If you've always wanted to play a musical instrument, or dance, or learn to sail, enroll in a class. Even if you don't think you have the talent or the ability, try it and see what happens.

What it really boils down to is this: you can do things in the same old way you've always done them, which is safe and secure, but also a little bit dull and boring, or you can try something new and different. You may learn something, and you may have some fun. So why not go for the fun?

Meditation

Contacting Your Creativity

$\mathscr{H}$ ere is a meditation to help you get in touch with your creativity. In this meditation, let your imagination open, and trust whatever comes to you. Enjoy it.

Find a comfortable place to sit or lie down. Close your eyes.

Relax.... Take a deep breath, and as you exhale, relax your body.... Take another deep breath, and as you exhale, relax your body more deeply.... Take another deep breath, and as you exhale, relax your body completely.... Feel the energy flowing freely through your body as you breathe....

As you inhale, imagine that you're breathing in the life force of the universe. Imagine it coming into every cell of your body. . . . As you exhale, release all the old limitations, fears, and doubt that you no longer need. Every time you exhale, you release the old and make room for the new. . . . And as you inhale, you bring in fresh, creative energy. . . .

Take another deep breath, and as you exhale, relax your mind. . . . Imagine that all your old, limited ideas about yourself are floating away. Imagine that all your old conditioning and programming about who you are and who you aren't, about what you can do and what you can't do, are all dissolving and floating away. You are an unlimited being, and you are now open to new ideas, new feelings, and new inspirations. . . .

Take another deep breath, and as you exhale, allow your awareness to move into a deep place inside of you. . . . With each breath imagine going deeper and deeper, until you come to rest in a quiet place inside. . . .

Now imagine that you are walking down a beautiful path toward your inner sanctuary. . . . As you walk down the path toward your sanctuary, you are feeling very open and alive, almost like a new person, ready to have new experiences and new adventures, and to discover something new about yourself. . . .

Enter your sanctuary and take a few moments to experience being there.... Notice what's in your sanctuary, how it looks, how it feels. You may find there's something different about it today, or it may be the same as usual. ... Allow yourself to feel the peace and nurturing and safety of being in your sanctuary.... Find a place to sit down and be comfortable....

Today we're going to invite your creative being, the most creative part of yourself, to come into your sanctuary with you. Look toward the entrance of your sanctuary and begin to sense or visualize your creative being coming down the path.... This is some part of you that is very creative. It may be a part that you've been in touch with before, or it may be some part of you that you've never seen or experienced before. Just trust whatever comes to you in your imagination now....

As this creative being comes into your sanctuary, begin to see or sense who it is, what it looks like.... It could be a person, a man or woman, an animal, a color or shape, or anything that comes to your mind.... Notice the details about your creative being. Let yourself be open to its appearing in whatever way it wishes....

Now your creative being comes toward you and you make contact with each other.... Allow yourself to feel the energy of this creative being. . . . Ask the being what message it has for you or what it wants to tell you or communicate to you, whether in words or in any other way. . . . Ask your creative being what it most wants to do, how it wants to express itself in your life. . . . Also ask your creative being how it already expresses itself in your life. . . . Ask if there's anything it would like to do with you right now, and go ahead and be together in whatever way feels good or right. . . .

Your creative being wants to take you somewhere. Allow yourself to be guided by your creative being on a little journey through your sanctuary, to an area that you've never seen before. . . . In this new place there is a beautiful pool of clear, warm water. Your creative being lets you know that this is a pool of your own creative energy. Take your clothes off and slowly enter the pool and let yourself float in the warm water. . . .

As you float in the pool, look up and watch the sky gradually become a night sky, with bright stars shining. . . . You see one star that's particularly bright, and you know that this is your special star. . . . The star has something to tell you about the purpose of your life at this time. Listen to what the star has to say to you. . . .

When you feel ready to emerge from the pool, step out of the water. . . . You will find that your clothes have disappeared and your creative being has brought you new clothes that are very special and magical. Your creative being dresses you in these new clothes. . . . The clothes feel wonderful, as though they are expressing an essence of who you are. Let yourself move freely, and just notice how your body feels in these clothes. . . . If it feels right to you, you might even dance with your creative being in a dance that feels like a true expression of how you feel. . . .

When you feel complete, you and your creative being move back to your familiar place in the sanctuary. . . . Ask if there are any steps your creative being wants you to take in your life right now. . . . Then ask if there's anything further your creative being wants to express to you at this time. . . .

If you want to stay in your sanctuary and stay with your creative being, you may continue to do so as long as you desire. . . . If you're ready to leave, you and your creative being can walk together out of the sanctuary and up the path. . . . As you walk up the path, feel your creative being with you, as a part of you that you can invoke in your life anytime you wish. . . .

Become aware of your body and of your presence in the room. . . . When you feel ready, open your eyes and come back into the room.

If you wish, take some paint, colored pens, or crayons and make a picture of your creative being and/or of your inner sanctuary. Don't worry about how perfect or imperfect the picture is. Let your creative inner child draw the picture. Hang it on your wall or put it in your notebook to help you remember and express that creativity within you.

From the audio *Meditations* by Shakti Gawain.

Developing Intuition

*T*here is a universal, intelligent life force that exists within everyone and everything. It resides within each one of us as a deep wisdom, an inner knowing. We can access this wonderful source of knowledge and wisdom through our intuition, a kind of inner sense that tells us what feels right and true for us at any given moment.

Many people who are not accustomed to being consciously in touch with their intuition imagine that it is a mysterious force that would come to them through some transcendent mystical experience. In fact, our intuition is a very practical, down-to-earth tool that is always available to help us deal with the decisions, problems, and challenges of our daily lives. One way that we often describe an intuitive prompting is as a "gut feeling" or a "hunch."

Intuition is a natural thing. We are all born with it. Young children are very intuitive, although they are often trained out of it early in life.

We are accustomed to thinking that some people are intuitive and some aren't. Women are generally considered to be more intuitive than men, for example. Yet many men follow their hunches on a regular basis. In reality, we are all potentially intuitive. Some of us consciously develop this ability, while a majority of us learn to disregard and deny it. Still, many people are unconsciously following their intuition frequently without realizing it.

Fortunately, with some practice most of us can re-claim and develop our natural intuitive abilities. We can learn to be in touch with our intuition, to follow it, and to allow it to become a powerful guide in our lives.

In many cultures, including most of the indigenous peoples of the world, intuition is acknowledged, re-spected, and honored as a natural and important as-pect of life. Every moment of daily life is guided by a strong sense of connection to the universal creative force. These societies create powerful rituals, such as group counsels, dream sharing, chants, dances, and vision quests that support their connection to the inner, intuitive realms. Individuals within those cul-tures learn to trust and follow their own inner sense of truth and offer it as their wisdom to others. They have a profound sense of the interconnectedness of all life.

Our modern Western culture, on the other hand, does not always acknowledge the validity or even the existence of intuition. We respect, honor, and develop the rational aspect of our nature and, at least until recently, have disregarded and discounted the intuitive side.

Our school system reflects and reinforces this bias. It focuses almost exclusively on developing our left brain, rational abilities and mostly ignores the development of the right brain, intuitive, holistic, creative capacities. We often see the same bias in the business world. Only in recent years have some schools and businesses begun to encourage creativity and progressive thinking.

The rational mind is like a computer — it processes the input it receives and calculates logical conclusions based on this information. The rational mind is finite; it can only compute the data that it has received directly from the external world. In other words, our rational minds can only operate on the basis of the direct experience each of us has had in this lifetime — the knowledge we have gained through our five senses.

The intuitive mind, on the other hand, seems to have access to an infinite supply of information, including information that we have not gathered directly through personal experience. It appears to be able to tap into a deep storehouse of knowledge and wisdom — the universal mind. It is also able to sort out this information and supply us with exactly what we need, when we need it. Although the message may come through a bit at a time, if we learn to follow this flow of information step-by-step, the necessary course of action will be revealed. As we learn to rely on this guidance, life takes on a flowing, effortless quality. Our life, feelings, and actions interweave harmoniously with those of others around us.

In suggesting that our intuition needs to be the guiding force in our lives, I am not attempting to disregard or eliminate the intellect. Our rational faculty is a very powerful tool that can help us organize, understand, and learn from our experiences, so of course it is important to educate our minds and develop our intellectual capacities. However, if we attempt to direct our life primarily from our intellect, we are likely to miss out on a great deal. In my experience, it works best to balance and integrate logic with intuition.

Many of us have programmed our intellect to doubt our intuition. When an intuitive feeling arises, our rational minds immediately say, "I don't think that will work," or "what a foolish idea," and the intuition is disregarded. We must train our intellect to respect and listen to the intuitive voice. We must allow the intuitive voice to find expression.

Fortunately it doesn't take a long time or a lot of work to develop our intuitive abilities. In fact, I've facilitated thousands of people in this process and I've found that with a little explanation and practice, the vast majority of them are able to get in touch with their intuition and begin following it on a regular basis. From there, the whole process of balancing logic with intuition happens easily and naturally.

Developing your intuitive ability begins with paying attention to what's going on inside of you so that you can become aware of these inner dialogues and catch them when they are happening, or shortly afterward. As you become more aware of your inner process, you will begin to notice the intuitive feelings as they pop up, and you will then be able to deal with them more consciously.

One of the keys to getting in touch with your intuition is learning to relax your mind and relax your body sufficiently so that you can allow your attention to move out of your head and literally "drop down" into a deeper place in your body, closer to where your gut feelings reside. Simply letting your awareness move into a deeper place in your body in this way is tremendously helpful in opening the door to intuition.

In the modern world, we are so accustomed to living in a state of stress that many of us don't really know how to relax physically, mentally, and emotionally except when we're sleeping (and some of us not even then!).

Once you have a little practice in relaxing, going inside, asking for an intuitive message, and paying attention to what comes to you either then or later, you can begin to integrate the process more naturally into your daily life.

In the middle of a busy day you may not have time to sit down and do a deep meditation. However, you can learn to "check in" with your intuition on a regular basis throughout the day.

In order to do this, you need to develop the habit of pausing every now and then and taking a moment to notice what is going on inside of you.

Meditation

Quick Intuitive Check-In

*H*ere is a quick, simple exercise that can help you touch into your intuition even in the midst of a lot of activity. You can do this at your desk, or in a parked car briefly before or after you drive somewhere.

One excellent way to ensure a moment of quiet and privacy is to go into the bathroom to do this exercise. Of course, it's even better if you can take a minute to walk or sit outdoors; however, don't wait for that time if it is not going to happen easily. Just do it whenever and wherever you can.

Close your eyes and take a deep breath, exhaling slowly. . . . Notice what's on your mind, what you've

been thinking about. . . . Notice how your body is feeling right now. How are you feeling emotionally? Do
you feel like you are more or less "in the flow," following your own energy, or do you feel stressed,
conflicted, out of sorts?

Take another deep breath, exhale slowly, and let your
awareness move into a deep place inside. . . . Is there
anything you need to pay attention to that would help
you feel more connected to yourself? Any gut feeling you
need to be aware of? Whether or not you get any specific information or awareness, enjoy a moment of rest
before you carry on. . . .

It doesn't matter too much what happens for you
when you do this exercise. Just the fact that you are
taking a moment to be with yourself and tune in on a
deeper level will be very healing, and chances are that
it will help you get more into the present moment.
The more present and connected with ourselves we
are, the more likely we are to notice and follow our
intuitive feelings, and the more effective we are likely
to be in whatever we do.

To assist you in remembering to do this exercise, you
can put little reminders where you are likely to see
them around your work area and your home. A re-
minder can take the form of a little note to yourself, a

poem, a picture, or an object that symbolizes or con-
veys to you a feeling of connecting to your intuition.
You may want to put your reminders in different
places every now and then, so that the reminders remain fresh and new and don't get overlooked and
begin to blend into their surroundings.

Remember that our intuitive wisdom is always there
inside of us and available. We may not always be able
to access it, usually because we are too caught up in
our activities, our minds, or our emotions. That's
okay; it's just part of the cycles that we go through.

If you do this exercise or anything similar to it often,
you will begin to build a relationship with your intuitive self and it will come through to you more and
more frequently and clearly.

If we can develop the habit of checking our intuitive
messages, at least as often as most of us check our telephone messages, we'll be in great shape!

Applying the Intuitive Check-In

You can also apply the intuitive check-in to im-
mediate situations. Here's an example.

A few days ago one of my clients was driving to
work and she got a flat tire. Her first impulse was to call

her mom to come rescue her, but something inside her said, "pause a moment, help is right there." She listened to this feeling, paused for a moment, observed her surroundings, and within minutes was approached by a young couple willing and able to help her. Within twenty minutes she was on her way again.

If we can get into the habit of pausing and checking in with our inner guidance, we will often find answers to many of our questions throughout the day.

From the book *Developing Intuition: Practical Guidance for Daily Life* by Shakti Gawain.

Integration and Balance

*W*e are living in a profoundly exciting yet deeply challenging time. Humanity as a whole, and each of us as individuals, are confronted with the fact that the ways we have been accustomed to living no longer work for us, or our planet. For our own personal satisfaction, we need to find ways to develop and express all aspects of who we are. And for the common good, we have to find a way to live on earth with greater consciousness.

In order to do these things, we need to look honestly at ourselves, to recognize the areas of unconsciousness in our lives. We must learn how to heal the wounded places within us and nurture our own growth and development. Many of us are searching for insight, practical guidance, and tools that can support us in this process.

It has helped me greatly to understand that there are four very different aspects of life — the spiritual, mental, emotional, and physical. In order to find balance, wholeness, and fulfillment in our lives, we need to heal, develop, and integrate all four of these aspects within ourselves.

Our spiritual aspect is our inner essence, our soul, the part of us that exists beyond time and space. It connects us with the universal source and the oneness of all life. Developing our awareness of the spiritual level of our being allows us to experience a feeling of belonging in the universe, a deeper meaning and purpose in our lives, and a broader perspective than we have from our personality alone. The spiritual level provides a foundation for the development of the other levels.

Our mental aspect is our intellect, our ability to think and reason. The mental level of our existence consists of our thoughts, attitudes, beliefs, and values. Our minds can be our greatest gift, and at times our greatest curse. They can cause us terrible confusion or bring us profound understanding. Developing the mental level of our being allows us to think clearly, remain open-minded, yet discriminate intelligently. Our minds enable us to gather knowledge and wisdom from our life experience and from the world around us.

Our emotional aspect is our ability to experience life deeply, to relate to one another and the world on a feeling level. It's the part of us that seeks meaningful contact and connection with others. Developing the emotional level of our being allows us to feel the full range of the human experience, and find fulfillment in our relationships with ourselves and each other.

Our physical aspect is, of course, our physical body. It also includes our ability to survive and thrive in the material world. Developing the physical level of our being involves learning to take good care of our bodies, and to enjoy them. It also means developing the skills to live comfortably and effectively in the world.

All four of these levels of existence are equally important. In the long run, we can't afford to neglect any of them. If we want to feel whole and lead healthy, satisfying lives, we need to focus a certain amount of time and attention on healing and developing each aspect.

Most of us have had the opportunity to develop certain parts of ourselves more than others. Maybe we were actively discouraged from expressing certain aspects, or we simply did not know how. Some levels may need special healing because we were wounded or suffered trauma in those areas.

For example, if you were taught certain spiritual beliefs you eventually felt weren't right for you, and as a result rejected the entire spiritual side of life, you may have a wound on the spiritual level, which can be healed by developing your own personal way of relating to spirit. If you don't feel confident intellectually,

you may have a wound on the mental level. All of us
have suffered some degree of disappointment, hurt, or
pain that leave us emotionally wounded and in need of
healing. Many of us have certain physical weaknesses
that need special attention. We may lack the confidence to live successfully in the material world, in
which case we can heal ourselves by developing certain skills.

There is no one right way to carry out our healing
process. Everyone is different and follows a unique
path of development. We may proceed in developing
the four levels in any order, or all at once. Our lives
definitely guide us in this process. (You can find exercises and a more detailed discussion of healing the
four levels of existence in my book *The Four Levels of
Healing.*)

The ultimate goal is the integration of all four levels. As we follow our healing path, giving our attention
to each of the levels as the need arises, we find that the
four aspects — spiritual, mental, emotional, and physical — gradually become more integrated with one another. As we do this, we not only bring harmony and
wholeness into our own lives but we also help to bring
healing and balance to the world.

Meditation

Integration Meditation

*W*hat follows is a meditation to help you integrate the four levels of existence. This is a good exercise to do on a daily or regular basis.

Sit or lie down in a comfortable position with your back straight and supported. Close your eyes and relax. Take a deep breath, and as you exhale, let go of everything you don't need to focus on right now. Take another deep breath, and as you exhale, let your awareness move deep inside. . . . Keep breathing slowly and fully, and allow your attention to move deeper and deeper inside. Move deeper than your body, mind, or emotions, until you come to a quiet place inside. . . .

In this quiet place, open to feeling and experiencing your spiritual essence. Just sit quietly and invite your spirit in.... Whether or not you feel anything in particular, just assume it's there. Know that it is always with you at every moment of your life. In this place, you are one with all of creation.

Now move slowly to the mental level. Imagine yourself very mentally clear and alert.... Imagine that you believe in yourself, you have confidence in your power to create and manifest whatever you truly want in your life.... You believe that life is supporting you in every way.

Now check in with yourself on the emotional level. How are you feeling right now? Can you accept and be with your feelings? Imagine yourself feeling comfortable with all your emotions.... Know that as human beings we have many deep feelings that are gifts to help us take care of ourselves, to teach us about life. So imagine yourself respecting and honoring all your feelings and learning to express them appropriately and constructively....

Become aware of your physical body, and begin to sense how it feels. Give your body the love and appreciation it needs and deserves.... Imagine that you are learning to listen to your body and pay attention to what it needs and feels. You take good care of it, and as a result it feels healthy, fit, alive, and beautiful. Imagine feeling comfortable and happy in your body....

Now expand that feeling to your surroundings. Imagine yourself feeling comfortable and confident in the physical world, able to take good care of yourself and handle the practical aspects of life easily and efficiently.... Your environment reflects this — it is orderly and beautiful. Take a few minutes to imagine your day unfolding in a flowing and fulfilling way....

When you feel complete with this, slowly open your eyes, stretch gently, and go about your life.

From the book *The Four Levels of Healing: A Guide to Balancing the Spiritual, Mental, Emotional, and Physical Aspects of Life* by Shakti Gawain.

Our Relationships As Mirrors

On the transformational path we need to recognize that our relationships can be powerful mirrors, reflecting back to us what we need to learn. When we learn how to use these reflections, our relationships can become one of the most powerful avenues we have for becoming conscious.

Our primary relationship is really with ourselves. Each of us is involved in developing all aspects of our being and bringing them into relationship with one another — becoming whole. Our relationships with other people continually reflect exactly where we are in that process. For example, for many years I yearned to find the right man to be my life partner. I created many relationships with men who were unavailable or inappropriate in certain ways. Eventually, I realized they were reflecting my own inner ambivalence about committed relationship and the ways that I didn't truly love myself. It was only after I did some deep emotional healing work, learning to truly love and be committed to myself, that I met a wonderful man who is now my husband.

If we learn to see our relationships as the wonderfully accurate mirrors they are, revealing to us where we need to go with our own inner process, we can see much about ourselves that we would otherwise have a great deal of difficulty learning. Any and every relationship in our lives — with our friends, coworkers, neighbors, our children and other family members, as well as our primary partners — can be a reflection to us in this way. Even an encounter with a stranger can sometimes be an important learning experience.

To understand how this works, we need to remind ourselves that we each, through our individual consciousness, create and shape how we experience external reality. This is as true in our relationships as in every other area of our lives — the relationships we create and shape reflect back to us what we are holding within our consciousness. We draw to us and are drawn to people who match and reflect some aspect of ourselves.

Generally, we find that the easiest people to get along with are those who reflect aspects of ourselves that we feel comfortable with and accept. These are usually people who we consciously seek out or are drawn to in everyday friendship.

The people in our lives who make us uncomfortable, who annoy us, whom we feel judgmental or even combative toward, reflect parts of ourselves that we reject — usually aspects of our disowned parts, the shadow side of our personality.

Oftentimes we find ourselves attracted to our opposites — people who have developed opposite qualities from the ones we most identify with. In these relationships, we are unconsciously seeking to become whole, and we are drawn to people who express those energies that are undeveloped in our own personalities. On some level, we recognize that they have the potential to help us become more balanced.

Meditation

Using the Mirror of Relationship

*D*ifficulties we are having in our relationships often mirror parts of ourselves that we need to heal. Such difficulties may involve a family member, a close friend, a coworker, or even people with whom we have only a brief encounter, such as a clerk in a store.

If you are having difficulty with a present relationship, or if you frequently encounter certain kinds of difficult people — for example, a needy person or a person who doesn't respect your boundaries — take a moment to look closely at what they are reflecting. The following meditation will help you do that.

Begin by closing your eyes and relaxing for a few moments.... Then bring to mind a difficult relationship.... Think about what, exactly, bothers you about this person. What quality or trait does this person have that makes you uncomfortable or that you judge?

Once you have identified the quality or qualities that bother you, ask yourself what the positive aspect or essence of that quality might be. For example, if you see them as lazy, what could be the positive aspect of laziness? It could be the ability to relax....

Ask yourself how it might benefit you to develop a bit more of that quality in yourself.... Could it help you find more balance in your life? If you are judging someone as lazy, chances are you are a very active, driven type of person who could benefit from developing a greater ability to relax. This person is a mirror, reflecting the disowned quality of relaxation to you, so that you can become more aware of what you need to develop....

Here are some other examples: If you find someone too needy, they may be reflecting the disowned part of you that has emotional needs. You may be too identified with strength and self-sufficiency and need to get more in touch with your vulnerability. If you find someone too domineering, perhaps you are overly timid and need to develop more assertiveness. If you judge someone as selfish, it's possible that you are too giving.

Remember that you don't need to become like this person. They may be too far to the extreme or expressing themselves in a distorted way. However, you can use the discomfort of this relationship to help you discover the essential qualities you need to develop in order to feel more whole and fulfilled.

Once you have identified what quality this person is reflecting to you, imagine yourself having integrated more of that quality in yourself.... Imagine yourself more able to relax, for example, or more able to show your vulnerability in close relationships, or more assertive, or more able to receive....

From the book *The Path of Transformation: How Healing Ourselves Can Change the World* by Shakti Gawain.

Creating
True Prosperity

$\mathcal{W}$hat is prosperity? Take a minute and think about what the word means to you. I find that most people think prosperity would be having plenty of money. But how much is plenty?

Unfortunately, most of us don't experience prosperity, no matter how much money we have. And the truth is, prosperity has less to do with money than most of us believe. So what is it, really? I believe that prosperity is the experience of having plenty of what we truly need and want in life, material and otherwise. Prosperity is an internal experience, not an external state. And it is an experience that is not tied to having a certain amount of money. While prosperity is in some ways related to money, it is not *caused* by money, and while no amount of financial wealth can guarantee an experience of prosperity, it is possible to experience prosperity at almost any level of income, except when we are unable to meet our basic physical needs. Problems exist at every level of income, and prosperity can exist at every level too.

Even if we recognize that prosperity isn't caused by money, we have to admit that in the modern world, prosperity and money are usually linked. So let's look at our understanding of and relationship with money.

There are three approaches to money and prosperity that I encounter frequently. The first one is the materialistic viewpoint. In the materialistic approach, money is the key to getting what we want in life. The focus is all external. We believe that our satisfaction and fulfillment come from the physical plane and money gives us the power to get what we want in the physical world. Prosperity is material wealth and the strategy for creating prosperity is to make more.

The second viewpoint is the transcendent, spiritual approach. In this philosophy, money represents the material world, which on some level is a trap, a prison, a seduction away from spirit. In many ways this viewpoint is the opposite of the material. The focus is completely internal. We believe that fulfillment comes from the spiritual plane and prosperity from simplifying our physical needs to the absolute minimum and looking toward our spiritual connection for gratification and fulfillment. A truly dedicated seeker renounces the world and even takes vows of poverty. Physical poverty brings spiritual prosperity, so the strategy for creating prosperity is needing less.

Then there's the approach that I call the new age viewpoint. In this philosophy we understand that the physical world mirrors our consciousness. Money reflects our beliefs and our thoughts, so unlimited wealth is available if we change our thinking and are willing to have it. In this attempt to bridge the inner and the outer, the strategy for creating prosperity is to change your thinking so that you can then have as much as you want.

All three of these viewpoints contain elements of truth and may be helpful or appropriate at certain times. But I believe that each of these is too limited to help most of us create true prosperity in our lives.

The materialistic approach can help us succeed in the physical world. The problem with this philosophy is that it focuses only on the external and denies the importance of the inner realms — our spiritual, our mental, and our emotional needs. It ultimately leads to a sense of emptiness and disappointment because no matter what we have outside, our inner needs are not necessarily being met.

The transcendent view offers an escape from the trap of materialism. It acknowledges our need to feel connected with spirit and to feel part of something larger than our individual physical existence. Unfortunately, in swinging to the opposite extreme, it creates another trap. It denies the importance of the physical and the emotional aspects of our being, and these are important parts of who we are. I find that most of us who try to follow the transcendent philosophy develop tremendous inner conflict. In pursuing our spiritual development, we're trying to rise above our human experience. We try not to want and not to need, and yet as human beings, we do need and we do want a great deal. We get pulled between our yearning for spiritual fulfillment and our human needs instead of trusting and honoring all of our deep needs and feelings.

The new age approach is on the right track in many ways. Our life does reflect our consciousness and the external world is our mirror. As we learn and grow and become more aware, our experience of external reality shifts to reflect the internal changes we make. So our relationship with money and our experience of prosperity definitely do mirror our internal process. However, the way this philosophy is generally understood and expressed, I believe, is far too simplistic and limited to address the real issues most of us encounter in our quest to create prosperity.

I'd like to present another viewpoint. It's a way of looking at money and prosperity that draws from all of these philosophies, but goes beyond them. This approach can give us a framework to understand and to use our relationship with money as a mirror, guiding us toward true prosperity.

Essentially, money is a symbol for energy. Everything in the universe is made of energy. Even physical objects that appear solid really aren't; if we look at them under a powerful microscope we see that they're actually made of vibrating particles. Our bodies, minds, emotions, and spirit all consist of energy. Money is a medium of exchange we've created to represent our creative energy. Money itself just consists of pieces of paper or metal (or plastic) with very little value. But we've decided to let it symbolize the energy that we exchange with one another. So you go out and work at whatever you do. You use your energy in a certain way and earn money for that. You may have used some of that money to buy this book, in exchange for the energy that I put into writing it, and that the publisher put into making it available to you.

Since money symbolizes energy, our financial affairs tend to reflect how our life energy is moving. When our creative energy is flowing freely, oftentimes our finances are as well. If our energy gets blocked, our money can too. Actually, everything going on in our life is a reflection of how our energy is moving. Our relationships, our health, all of these things reflect the flow of energy moving through us. Money is just another mirror, an incredibly useful one that reveals what is going on in our consciousness, what is and isn't working in our lives.

Our financial circumstances will reflect how we feel about the qualities we consciously or unconsciously associate with money. So on a deep level, if we feel unworthy of success or happiness we may unconsciously prevent ourselves from having much money. Or, if we're deeply insecure and money represents power and status, we may be compulsively driven to accumulate wealth in the hope that it will bring us the security and validation we yearn for.

Having money allows us to do things, to get things, to make things happen. Money gives us a certain ability to make an impact on the world around us. So our relationship with money reflects how we feel about our power to have an effect on the world. Since money is a mirror of our consciousness, the more comfortable we are with being powerful, the more money we are likely to create in our lives. Many of us have issues with power and these are likely to be reflected in our relationship with money. In fact, if you have chronic financial problems, I strongly suggest that you take a deep, honest look at your feelings about power. If we're afraid of our power, we may unconsciously keep ourselves from making much money, since to have money is to have power. In fact, struggling with financial need is a very effective way to keep ourselves feeling powerless, and thereby avoid the risks we may associate with power.

Once we're committed to a path of consciousness growth, we generally only create as much money in our lives as we can manage responsibly — enough to live on and support our process without distracting us or jeopardizing our journey. As our ability to handle energy and power matures, we tend to generate more money. We usually receive exactly the amount of money we need in order to do the things that are truly right for us. To the degree that we follow our hearts and souls, we will experience this flow of money in our lives as true financial prosperity.

I see seven steps on the road to an increasing sense of prosperity. These aren't steps that are necessarily taken in any particular order; they describe different elements of the journey. We each have our own unique path. We may focus on each of these elements at various times and in various ways. At times we may even work on all of them at once.

Step one is gratitude. Whether or not we feel really prosperous at the moment, the truth is that most of us in modern society are enormously prosperous materially and in many other ways. Whatever our individual troubles and challenges may be, it's important to pause every now and then and appreciate all that we have on every level. We need to literally count our blessings, give thanks for them, allow ourselves to enjoy them and relish the experience of prosperity we already have.

Step two is awareness. We all have certain ideas, attitudes, core beliefs, and emotional patterns that limit our experience of prosperity. Deep feelings of unworthiness, a sense of scarcity, fear of failure or success, conflicting feelings and beliefs about money, and many other issues can block our growth and fulfillment. Most of these beliefs and patterns are initially unconscious. We're not aware of them and yet they control our lives. The moment we begin to consciously recognize them, we're on the road to having real choice about how we live.

Step three is healing. We can't force ourselves to change, but we can support and enhance the process of change that we're going through. Of course, there are many ways to go about supporting our healing and development. Different tools and techniques are appropriate and helpful at different times in our journey, and certain things are helpful to some people and not to others. I believe we know intuitively what is right for us at any given moment and can learn to trust and follow that inner sense. The work of healing needs to be done on all levels of our existence, the spiritual, the mental, the emotional, and the physical. I wish I could offer a simple magic formula for healing but there is no quick and easy way, for on a deep level, this is truly our life's work. We need to surrender to the fact that life is an ongoing adventure in healing and growth — and learn to enjoy the ride. I also feel that it's very important to get help and support from others as we need it along the way. A good therapist, teacher, healer, support group, or wise friend or mentor can all be valuable resources for our healing process.

Step four is following your truth. We all have within us a deep sense of what we need and what is right and true for us. To access this we need to pay attention to our feelings and our intuition. We need to learn to listen deeply to ourselves and to trust what we hear. We need to risk acting on what we feel to be true. Even if we make mistakes, we must do this in order to learn and to grow. With some practice, you can easily learn to develop your ability to receive and to follow your inner guidance.

Step five is creating a vision. What would a truly prosperous life look and feel like for you? Where and how would you like to live? How would you feel about yourself? How would your body feel? What would your relationships be like? What kind of work or creative expression would you have? What other aspects of your lifestyle can you imagine? How would a typical day in your life unfold? How would you feel at the end of your day? It's important to imagine how you would like things to be. Our imagination is a powerful creative tool. Vividly imagining something often opens the door to manifesting it.

Step six is setting goals. Once you have a sense of your overall vision for a truly prosperous life, you can set some specific goals. There are times in life when it is helpful to set goals, and other times when it's best to let go of goals for a time and just see where life takes you. So if you check in with yourself and it doesn't feel right, let it go for now. If it feels exciting and fun, or helpful, then go ahead and give it a try. Goals can help us gain clarity, inspiration, and focus. However, they can also work against us if we hold on to them too tightly, or try too hard to make them happen. So, try to let go of your attachment to having them happen in a certain way, or certain time. Don't worry about how to make them happen, let the higher creative power handle the details. Hold your goals lightly and allow them to change and evolve as you do. You may find that certain things are going as you hoped while others aren't. You may even find that your whole life is going in a different direction than you expected. Remember that our souls have a purpose in this life that we may not fully understand yet, and everything that happens to us is a part of our soul's journey. Learn from everything that comes your way. Continue to follow your intuitive sense. If a certain goal is right for you it will unfold naturally from this process. Let your inner guidance show you the way.

Step seven is sharing your gifts. As you follow these steps you will find yourself naturally expressing and developing the special talents and abilities that you brought into this life. When you follow your heart and are committed to your healing and growth, you simply can't help becoming more and more of who you were meant to be. Unless we are blocked in our ability to succeed or receive, life always rewards us appropriately for what we give. Through answering what calls us we develop our right livelihood. Essentially, the universe pays us to be ourselves as fully as possible! The opportunity to share our gifts and thereby make a difference in the world is one of the most profoundly fulfilling experiences we can have in life, and an essential ingredient in creating true prosperity.

Remember that none of us exists in a vacuum. We are powerfully affected by the world around us and we have an equally powerful effect on the world, whether or not we realize it. We are an integral part of the whole. We can only have a truly prosperous life to the extent that our world is prosperous. And our world can only be truly prosperous when we learn how to honor and respect the earth we live on and all the other beings, human and otherwise, who live here as well. I believe that those of us fortunate enough to live in circumstances where we have the luxury of pursuing personal growth have a responsibility to use what we learn to make the world a healthier, more prosperous place for all. Since we're all ultimately part of one consciousness, the most effective way to do that is to take responsibility for our own healing. The more conscious and balanced we become, the more we live in integrity and follow our truth, the more healing we bring to the world. We need to ask our inner guidance if there are specific actions we need to take to make our contribution to the world.

Meditation

Experiencing Gratitude

*T*he meditations that follow are designed to guide you in the steps on your path, and to support an ever expanding experience of true prosperity. The first meditation can help you develop appreciation and gratitude for the prosperity you are already experiencing in your life. The second meditation can help you increase your experience of prosperity by getting in touch with your true needs and desires and imagining them coming true.

To begin, find a quiet, peaceful place where you know that you will not be disturbed. Get in a comfortable position, either sitting up with your back supported so that you can truly relax and be comfortable, or lying down on your back, perhaps with a pillow under your knees, once again so that you can be completely comfortable and relaxed. Close your eyes, take a deep breath, and as you exhale, relax your body. Take another deep breath and as you exhale, relax your body a little bit more. As you take another deep breath and exhale, relax your body as deeply and completely as you can. . . .

Let your awareness move through your body slowly, and notice if there's any place in your body that is feeling tight or tense, or holding on. If so, put your attention into that place, gently breathe into that area, and imagine allowing all excess tension or energy that you don't need to release and drain down into the floor and be completely released from your body. . . . Continue to breathe slowly, deeply, in a natural, easy way. . . .

Take another deep breath and as you exhale, relax your mind. . . . Let your thoughts just float away. . . . As each new thought comes up in your mind, let it go and float away as well. Imagine letting your mind slow down and become quiet. . . . Keep bringing your attention back to your body relaxing and your breath as you slowly inhale and exhale. Take another deep breath and as you exhale, let your awareness begin to move deep inside of you. With every exhalation, move a little deeper, a little deeper, and a little deeper, until you come to rest in the deepest, quietest place that you can find, deep in the core of your being....

Now I'd like you to begin to think of everything in your life that you appreciate and feel grateful for at this time, starting with your body and your health. Think of anything in the area of health and your body that you appreciate, anything that you feel grateful for.... And just bring each of those things to your mind and take a moment to be with that thought or that feeling or that image....

Once you've done that, think about anything in your life in the area of your relationships that you feel grateful for, and remember this can be in any aspect of your relationships — your friends, your family, your romantic partner or spouse, your children. Bring to mind anything that you can think of that you feel grateful for at this time in your life in the area of relationships.... And again, just let yourself be with that thought, feeling, or image for a few moments.... Give thanks for the prosperity that you are currently enjoying in the area of relationships in your life....

Now, bring to mind your home, and think about anything and everything that you appreciate about the home where you live.... Take the time to be with each thought, feeling, or image that comes to you about your home, and give thanks for the prosperity you are currently experiencing in relation to your home at this time in your life.

Next, bring to mind your work or your career, and look to see what you can appreciate right now in the area of work and career in your life.... Bring to mind anything that you feel grateful for about your work, and again take a few moments just to be with every thought, feeling, or image that comes to you.... And now, give thanks for the prosperity that you are enjoying at this time, whatever it might be, in the area of work and career.

Then think about the area of finances, and see if you can bring to mind something that you feel appreciative for at this time in your life in the area of money and finances.... Let yourself be with whatever thought, feeling, or image comes to you, what you can appreciate about the money and the financial situation in your life right now.... And give thanks for the level of financial prosperity you have created so far in your life.

Now, think about your creative expression, any particular interests, or enjoyments, or hobbies that you have in your life, and just notice if there's anything that you feel especially appreciative about or grateful for in this area of your life.... If so, bring that to your mind and be with that for a few moments....

Are there ways that you make a contribution to other people? Or to the world? Even in very, very small ways? Take a moment to appreciate and be grateful for the opportunity you have to serve other people and make a difference in the world....

And if there's anything else in your life that you can think of right now that you feel grateful for, take a moment to truly appreciate whatever that is, and give thanks for how that contributes to your experience of prosperity....

Now, get a sense of the whole picture, how many things you have in your life to feel grateful for, how much richness and prosperity you already have created in your life. Allow yourself to really open up and enjoy that; experience it as deeply as possible.... And don't forget to express your appreciation to everyone in your life who contributes to your experience of true prosperity....

To conclude this meditation, once again become aware of your body, noticing how your body feels right now.

Slowly take a few deep breaths, and when you're ready,
you can open your eyes, stretch your body a little bit,
and as you feel ready to, get up and go about your life,
remembering to appreciate and be grateful for your
true prosperity.

Meditation

Discovering and Envisioning
What You Need and Want

*T*ake a deep breath and as you exhale, let your awareness go inward. Keep breathing slowly and deeply, relaxing into the quietest place that you can find....

We are going to look at what we truly desire in each area of our lives.

Bring to mind your body and your health, and ask yourself in a deep place inside if there is anything that you truly desire that you don't already have in the area of physical health and well-being.... After you ask that question, quietly notice whatever thought, feeling, or image comes to you in response, and take a few moments just to be with that response.... Begin to imagine that whatever it is that you desire in this area of your life is happening, or has happened. What would it be like if you were experiencing the kind of health and well-being that you desire in your physical body? Let yourself imagine that now.... You might see a mental picture, or you might just get a feeling of it or a sense of it. Allow yourself to enjoy having what you truly desire.

When you feel complete with this, bring to mind the area of relationships, and ask in a deep place within yourself, What do I most need or desire in the area of relationship right now in my life? Sit quietly and notice whatever thought, feeling, or image comes to you in response to that question.... Now, let yourself begin to imagine having what it is you most desire.... Imagine it as if it were already true. Again you may see a mental picture, or you may simply think about it, or get a feeling or sense of it. Let yourself enjoy this .... This is something your heart is desiring; allow yourself to experience it.

When you feel complete with this, begin to think about your home. Ask in a deep place within if there's anything you truly need or desire in relation to your home. Again, notice whatever thought, feeling, or image arises in response to that question.... Allow yourself to imagine this as if it were happening, or as if it had already happened. Let yourself have the reality you desire in relation to your home, see what that feels like.

Now, turn your attention to the area of your work and your career, asking yourself deeply what you most need or desire in this area of your life at this time. Notice whatever thought, feeling, or image arises in answer to that question, and let yourself be with that.... Visualize the reality that you desire to create in the area of your work and your career. Imagine it as if it were already true, that whatever your heart is desiring is happening. And let yourself enjoy that experience....

Next, turn your attention to the area of money and finances. Ask yourself deeply, What do I need or truly desire to have in the financial area of my life? Let your answer come from a deep place within you.... And then allow yourself to begin imagining the money and financial aspect of your life working in the way that you deeply desire it to. Let yourself enjoy this experience.

When you feel complete with this, turn your attention to your creative expression, to any special interests you have, or to the area of play and recreation in your life. Ask yourself what you most need or want in any of these areas.... Notice what comes up when you ask

that question. Then let yourself begin imagining whatever it is you desire as if it were already true. . . .

Now turn your attention to the area of contributing to
the world and being of service, expressing your higher
purpose in the world. What do you most desire at this
time in your life in relation to making your contribution? Let yourself begin to imagine this as if it were already happening just the way you would like it to. . . .

If there is any other area of your life where you have a
strong need or desire, go through the same process.
Imagine what it is that you most want, as if it were already happening or had already happened. Let yourself have what you truly desire, and enjoy that feeling.

And last, but not least, now that we've envisioned our
prosperity on a personal level, let's turn our attention to
envisioning the healing of the world. Let yourself imagine
that the world is reflecting that sense of prosperity that
you were finding in yourself, and that as you discover and
develop your own experience of prosperity, you're sharing
that with the world around you. . . . Imagine in whatever
way comes to you that you are living
in a conscious, healthy, balanced, truly prosperous
world. . . .

When you feel complete with this meditation, once
again become aware of your physical body and notice

how your body is feeling right now. Slowly open your eyes. Rest quietly for a few moments. When you feel ready, gently stretch your body, slowly get up, and go forth into a life of increasing, true prosperity.

From the audio *Meditations for Creating True Property* by Shakti Gawain.

How We Can Change the World

$\mathscr{A}$ ll too often there seems to be a gulf between those working to effect political, social, and environmental reform and those committed to inner growth. But changing our lives and changing the world cannot be accomplished either by focusing exclusively on external solutions or by following a traditional transcendent, spiritual path in which the reality and importance of the physical world are minimized or denied. We need to choose an alternative — which I call the path of transformation — in which we commit ourselves to the integration of our spiritual and human aspects and learn to live as whole beings, in balance and fulfillment on the earth.

Because each of us makes a real and substantial difference on this planet, committing to our own consciousness journey is part of the transformation of the world. Integral to this transformation is an exploration of our thoughts, feelings, fears, and visions about our own personal futures and the future of the world.

Most of us will find that we have conflicting feelings. On one hand we feel hope, excitement, and a certain fascination with what the future may bring. On the other hand, we feel some doubt, fear, and perhaps even dread or despair. While our personal problems may feel confusing, the problems in the world — war, terrorism, disease, economic chaos — may well appear overwhelming.

The first step we must take in dealing with any challenge is to acknowledge what it is and how we feel about it. Only then can we find creative and effective solutions.

For a long time, I felt deeply troubled both by the difficulties I was experiencing in my own personal life and by the pain and suffering I saw in the world. Through many years of consciousness work, I had developed a strong connection with my spiritual self. From that perspective I could see the perfection of the whole process; I had a strong faith that there was meaning and purpose in it all and that it would all work out well eventually. The human part of me felt more unsure; on the emotional level I had fears and doubts about my own future and the future of the planet. I wondered if my own personal needs would ever get fulfilled, much less the needs of all the beings on this Earth.

As my healing process has deepened and continued, I have found a great deal more integration within myself, and my life is gradually becoming more balanced and satisfying. Do I get stuck and feel frustrated? Yes, frequently! But not as profoundly or as lengthily as before.

Along with my own healing has come a stronger sense of trust in the healing process going on in our world. I still feel pangs of fear and doubt sometimes when I am forced to confront some of the more upsetting aspects of our current reality. I expect that many external circumstances may get worse as old orders crumble. Yet deep inside, I feel more strongly than ever before that we are participants in an amazing evolutionary and transformational process.

The meditations that follow will help you get in touch with some of your own thoughts and feelings about your personal future and the future of our world. While the first exercise explores your current sense of things, the second invites you to pay special attention to your most creative fantasies, developing your vision and being as expansive as you'd like.

Meditation

What Is Your Vision
of the Future?

*S*it comfortably in a quiet place. If you wish, have a pen and paper or your journal within easy reach. Close your eyes and take a few slow, deep breaths. Take a moment to relax.... Then ask yourself, "What is my vision of the future? How do I feel about it?"

First, focus your attention on how you see, think, and feel about your own personal future. How do you imagine your future prospects in your career, your finances, your relationships, your family, friends, your physical health and fitness (including how you feel about your aging process), and your overall personal well-being?

Just sit quietly and note whatever thoughts, feelings, and images come up for you.... Try to be very honest with yourself and acknowledge all the thoughts and feelings you have about these things, both positive and negative....

Some of your inner responses to these questions might seem contradictory or confusing. For example, you might simultaneously have both positive and negative feelings about the same thing. That's perfectly natural and quite okay. Just acknowledge the full range of your feelings.

Now, expand your focus to imagine the future of your community, your country, humanity, the natural environment, the planet.... Just notice the images, thoughts, and feelings that come to you when you ask yourself to imagine the future of the world.... Again, try to be as honest as you can, and don't worry if your inner responses seem somewhat contradictory or confusing. For example, you might find yourself thinking, "There's so much potential for positive changes...but I wonder if we will destroy ourselves before we get a chance to make those changes!"

When you feel complete with the exercise, open your eyes. If you wish, take your pen and paper or your journal and write down as much as you can about what came to you as you imagined your personal future and the future of our planet. If you prefer, use colored pens or crayons and draw your images and feelings.

Meditation

Envisioning the Future Together

*G*et in a comfortable position with your pen and paper, journal, crayons, or whatever tools you'd like within easy reach. Close your eyes, and take a few slow, deep breaths. Let your awareness move into a quiet place deep inside of you. . . . Ask yourself, "What is my vision of the future?"

First, focus your attention on imagining your own personal future as you would most like it to be. If you're not quite sure how you want it to be, just allow yourself to go with one fantasy about it, knowing that you can change it whenever you want to. . . . Imagine your relationship with yourself as fulfilling as possible on all levels — spiritual, mental, emotional, and physical. Imagine everything in your life reflecting the balance

and harmony within your own being — your relationship, your work, your finances, your living situation,
your creative pursuits. Allow them all to be wonderfully successful and satisfying. . . .

Now expand your focus to imagine the future of the
world around you — your community, your country,
humanity, the natural environment, our planet. Allow
them all to reflect the integration and wholeness you
have found within yourself. . . . Imagine the new world
emerging and developing in a healthy, balanced, expansive way. Really let your imagination soar. Envi-
sion the world as you would love it to be.

When you feel complete with this process, open your
eyes. If you wish, write or draw your vision.

From the book *The Path of Transformation: How Healing Ourselves
Can Change the World* by Shakti Gawain.

About the Author

*S*hakti Gawain is the best-selling author of *Creative Visualization, Living in the Light, The Path of Transformation, Creating True Prosperity, Developing Intuition,* and several other books. A warm, articulate, and inspiring teacher, Shakti leads workshops internationally. For more than twenty years, she has facilitated thousands of people in learning to trust and act on their own inner truth, thus releasing and developing their creativity in every area of their lives.

Shakti and her husband, Jim Burns, make their home in Mill Valley, California, and on the island of Kauai.

For Information about Shakti Gawain's
workshops and products:
Phone: (415) 388-7195
E-mail: staff@shaktigawain.com
www.shaktigawain.com